"Being a teenager is hard! Being the parent of a teenager is equally hard! I can't imagine anyone better at helping teens and their parents navigate this season of life than Jim Burns. *Understanding Your Teen* is filled with practical wisdom and great stories. Philip and I have known Jim for decades, and his wisdom on family dynamics has been a great help to us personally as well as to our church, Oasis. If you are doing your best to understand your teenager, or if you know someone who is, then I can't suggest strongly enough that you need this book!"

**Holly Wagner,** pastor, Oasis Church, author of *Find Your Brave*

"I can't think of any twenty-first–century leader who has earned more right to speak to the topic of parent-teen relationships than Jim Burns! His sage insights come from his highly successful decades of being in the youth ministry trenches like few others. If you are the parent of a teenager, disregard this book at your own peril."

**Jeanne Mayo,** executive director of youth and young adult outreach, Victory World Church, Atlanta

"Once again, Jim Burns has written a practical, user-friendly guide for parents who are asking how to handle the predictable—and in some cases, not so predictable—issues that arise in the course of navigating the teen years. It will point parents in the right direction, keep them on the straight path, and bolster their parenting confidence."

**John Rosemond,** family psychologist, author of *Parenting by the Book*

"'So, even though we were all teenagers once, in a very real way we were never the age of today's teens.' That sentence is so Jim Burns. A little counterintuitive perhaps, but right on the money. Of course Jim doesn't just leave you hanging with those pithy statements. Jim applies all his experience, wisdom, and communication savvy to help you understand exactly what he means. Pretty soon you'll be quoting Jim Burns too (just like I've been doing for years). Simply put, nobody is more qualified to write a book for parents about teenagers. He's been there, done that—and he's been doing it for years. He covers key developmental issues but doesn't dwell on them or keep restating the obvious. He gets to the good stuff right away: great advice, insights, and practical how-tos for parents who want to succeed with their kids and see them grow into capable, well-adjusted, fun-to-be-around grownups."

**Wayne Rice,** cofounder, Youth Specialties, and conference director, the Legacy Coalition

"Jim Burns is a life-giving blend of encouragement and wisdom for all parents of teenagers. *Understanding Your Teen* will quickly become one of your go-to books as you navigate the highs and lows of adolescence."

**Kara Powell,** executive director of the Fuller Youth Institute, coauthor of *Growing Young*

"I don't know anyone I trust more to help me with my teens or you with yours than Jim Burns. He has spent his life studying teens and the youth culture helping parents make sense of it all. This book is the culmination of that work; I couldn't recommend it more. Loving and parenting your teen well begins with understanding them, and this is the resource that will get you there."

**Ron L. Deal,** speaker, therapist, and author of *The Smart Stepfamily* and *The Smart Stepmom*

"This really is the very best book I've ever read on parenting teenagers. It combines biblical wisdom, experience, discernment, and a heart attitude that builds relationships with our teenagers rather than driving them away, while setting clear expectations and boundaries. It addresses the most troubling and difficult areas of parenting teens without clichés or platitudes. It is absolutely the most practical and helpful book for youth workers, parents, and grandparents of teens I've come across. I highly recommend it!"

**Chip Ingram,** senior pastor, Venture Christian Church, and teaching pastor, Living on the Edge Ministry

"There is no such thing as a perfect parent, but there can be an informed and intentional parent . . . and this book will help. If you want guidance navigating the minefields of adolescence, this is your guide. Pick it up, digest, and you'll soon learn you're not alone in your journey. Practical help is waiting for you."

**Doug Fields,** author, *Purpose Driven Youth Ministry*

"As a lifelong youth worker, I'd always suspected that parenting teenagers wasn't easy; but after the fits and starts, joys and anxieties of parenting two of my own, I'm convinced that parenting teenagers is the single most difficult task in the universe. But like most difficult tasks, parenting teens can be immeasurably rewarding. What we all need—and what Jim Burns provides in this helpful book—is a wise traveling companion."

**Mark Oestreicher,** partner in the Youth Cartel, author of *Understanding Your Young Teen*

"The new book from Jim Burns, *Understanding Your Teen*, is sure to become a classic for parents whose hearts desire is to help shape their teen's character while facing and dealing with the realities of today's world. Jim will not only educate you, he will also give you the practical tools you need to help your teen make wise choices while maintaining a strong relationship that may be your lifeline for the future."

**David and Claudia Arp,** authors of *Suddenly They're 13*

"Jim Burns consistently delivers concise yet practical helps for parents and youth workers, and *Understanding Your Teen* is no exception. This is a must-read for anyone who intends to influence their children toward God's best."

**Wayne Cordeiro,** New Hope International

"As a father of seven children with ages ranging from three to twenty, I need all the help I can get—especially in building a closer relationship with my teenagers. Sometimes when I read a parenting book, I come away feeling discouraged because of all the ways I am falling short. Not this time! This book is packed with honest, biblically grounded conversations about the issues my teens are facing. This book will encourage you to keep connecting with the heart your teen."

**Rob Rienow,** founder of Visionary Family Ministries

"There's never been a more difficult time to raise teenagers. Not only are the teen years often fraught with angst and confusion—for kids and parents alike!—but also today's kids are facing challenges unique to their generation. In this volume, Jim Burns is placing an arm around stressed-out parents and showing them how to guide their teens toward adulthood with grace, wisdom, and compassion."

**Jim Daly,** president, Focus on the Family

"Don't believe the idea that the teenage years are something to dread! As the parent of two teens, I am so grateful for my friend Jim Burns and *Understanding Your Teen*. While today's kids face challenges that no other generation has faced, these years can also be wonderful—and this book shows us how!"

**Shaunti Feldhahn,** author of *For Women Only* and *For Parents Only*

"The family is the seedbed that best nourishes spiritual growth. When that soil is fertile with the grace and nutrients of Christian nurture, it provides the best environment for young people to grow into healthy, capable, spiritually fruitful human beings. Jim Burns is a guy who has been cultivating this soil for a long time. You'll appreciate the practical ideas in this book. Clearly, this is a writer not afraid to get down and dirty into the mud, mess, and wonder of raising healthy teenagers. With just the right combination of practical wisdom, 'can we talk here?' realism, and Christ-centered hopefulness, Jim gives us a wonderful resource for growing teenagers into young adults."

**Duffy Robbins,** professor of youth ministry, Eastern University

"*Understanding Your Teen* is a must-have for any parent! It is also a great resource for anyone who works with young people. Dr. Burns peels back the layers of adolescence and gives an inside glimpse into the perspective and world of teens. This book truly covers it all!"

**Albert Tate,** lead pastor, Fellowship Monrovia

"A lot of people understand teens but they don't know how to help you guide and lead yours. Jim does. My wife and I have two teens in college and two at home, and Jim's books such as The Purity Code have helped us greatly mold their characters—but this is a book that covers so much more. Anyone with a teenager (or someone acting like one) will benefit greatly from the wisest mind I know when it comes the challenge of raising great teenagers into outstanding adults."

**Steve Arterburn,** president, New Life Ministries

"*Understanding Your Teen* offers a lifetime of wisdom and insight for every parent, educator, and youth worker. Jim knows kids, parenting, marriage, and the family like few others, and in this book he brings important perspectives to some of the most vital current issues. A great resource for a couple, small group, or ministry leadership team."

**Chap Clark,** author, *Hurt 2.0: Inside the World of Today's Teenagers,* and professor of youth, family, and culture, Fuller Theological Seminary

"Parenting is complicated . . . but the teen years can be about as stressful as they come. Jim brings a lifetime's worth of experience to this book on parenting teens. This book shows incredible insight into what the issues today actually are, and gives practical guidance on how to handle them. You'll be so grateful for this book."

**Carey Nieuwhof,** founding pastor, Connexus Church

"*Understanding Your* Teen is a lightning bolt that will enlighten and energize parents, educators, and ministers. Jim Burns has been one of the most heavy-hitting and winning coaches of all time, not at the Super Bowl or a national championship game, but in the most crucial arena of them all . . . empowering us so that we can empower our most cherished possessions, children and grandchildren."

**Jay Strack,** founder and president, Student Leadership University

"My wife and I just entered the parenting teens phase. Our desire is to influence, not control, our children during these foundational years. My go-to guy for all things parenting is Jim Burns. *Understanding Your Teen* is the first step toward influencing your teen. We fully support the message of this book."

**Ted Cunningham,** pastor, Woodland Hills Family Church, author, *Fun Loving You* and *Trophy Child*

# *Understanding*
# *Your Teen*

SHAPING THEIR CHARACTER,

FACING THEIR REALITIES

*Jim Burns*

IVP Books

An imprint of InterVarsity Press

Downers Grove, Illinois

InterVarsity Press
P.O. Box 1400, Downers Grove, IL 60515-1426
ivpress.com
email@ivpress.com

InterVarsity Press® is the book-publishing division of InterVarsity Christian Fellowship/USA®, a movement of students and faculty active on campus at hundreds of universities, colleges, and schools of nursing in the United States of America, and a member movement of the International Fellowship of Evangelical Students. For information about local and regional activities, visit intervarsity.org.

All Scripture quotations, unless otherwise indicated, are taken from The Holy Bible, New International Version®, NIV®. Copyright © 1973, 1978, 1984, 2011 by Biblica, Inc.™ Used by permission of Zondervan. All rights reserved worldwide. www.zondervan.com The "NIV" and "New International Version" are trademarks registered in the United States Patent and Trademark Office by Biblica, Inc.™

While any stories in this book are true, some names and identifying information may have been changed to protect the privacy of individuals.

Cover design: David Fassett
Interior design: Jeanna Wiggins
Images: chat bubble: ©chaluk/iStockphoto

ISBN 978-0-8308-4487-6 (print)
ISBN 978-0-8308-9183-2 (digital)

Printed in the United States of America ∞

InterVarsity Press is committed to ecological stewardship and to the conservation of natural resources in all our operations. This book was printed using sustainably sourced paper.

**Library of Congress Cataloging-in-Publication Data**
A catalog record for this book is available from the Library of Congress.

| **P** | 21 | 20 | 19 | 18 | 17 | 16 | 15 | 14 | 13 | 12 | 11 | 10 | 9 | 8 | 7 | 6 | 5 | 4 | 3 | 2 | 1 |
|---|---|---|---|---|---|---|---|---|---|---|---|---|---|---|---|---|---|---|---|---|---|
| **Y** | 35 | 34 | 33 | 32 | 31 | 30 | 29 | 28 | 27 | 26 | 25 | 24 | 23 | 22 | 21 | 20 | 19 | 18 | 17 | | |

*To Heather McGrath and Alisha Ballard*

Words truly cannot express my gratefulness
for your involvement in HomeWord. As I was writing
this book, I was thinking of your beautiful families.
You come alongside and encourage so many.
I am blessed to be one of them.

● ● ●

*To Wayne Rice*

You started the *Understanding Your
Teenager* movement, and I've had the privilege
to learn so much from you. Your handprint is all over
this book. Thank you for your friendship and vision
to help parents understand their teens.

● ● ●

*To Doug Fields*

One of my youth group kids
who has become the foremost leader
in the world of youth ministry. A friend and
partner in ministry whom I deeply
respect and admire.

# Contents

Preface. . . . . . . . . . . . . . . . . . . . . . . . .   1

## Part One: Parenting Teens to Become Responsible Adults

1 Understanding Your Teenager . . . . . . . . . . .   7

2 Learning the Developmental Stages of Adolescence . .   17

3 Shaping Behavior without Crushing Character . . .   29

4 Energizing Your Teen's Spiritual Life . . . . . . . .   41

5 Creating a Media-Safe Home . . . . . . . . . . .   53

6 Teaching Healthy Sexuality . . . . . . . . . . . .   67

7 Ending the Homework Hassle While
Preparing for College. . . . . . . . . . . . . . . .   81

8 Keeping the Communication Lines Open . . . . . .   91

9 Becoming Students of the Changing Culture . . . .  101

10 Finding Intimacy in Your Marriage as
You Raise Your Teen . . . . . . . . . . . . . . . .  113

11 Dealing with a Troubled Teen . . . . . . . . . . .  125

## Part Two: Common Teen Issues and What Parents Can Do

12 Bullying and Cyberbullying . . . . . . . . . . . .  141

13 Dating Violence . . . . . . . . . . . . . . . . . .  147

14 Depression . . . . . . . . . . . . . . . . . . . . . . 149

15 Dinnertime . . . . . . . . . . . . . . . . . . . . . 153

16 Driving . . . . . . . . . . . . . . . . . . . . . . . 157

17 Drug and Alcohol Use and Abuse . . . . . . . . . 163

18 Eating Disorders . . . . . . . . . . . . . . . . . . 171

19 Overweight and Obesity . . . . . . . . . . . . . . 175

20 Self-Injury . . . . . . . . . . . . . . . . . . . . . 179

21 Sexual Abuse . . . . . . . . . . . . . . . . . . . . 183

22 Sleep . . . . . . . . . . . . . . . . . . . . . . . . 189

23 Suicide . . . . . . . . . . . . . . . . . . . . . . . 193

24 Tragedy . . . . . . . . . . . . . . . . . . . . . . . 197

Conclusion . . . . . . . . . . . . . . . . . . . . . . . 201

Acknowledgments . . . . . . . . . . . . . . . . . . . . 203

Notes . . . . . . . . . . . . . . . . . . . . . . . . . . 205

# Preface

*IN MANY WAYS,* you are holding my life's work in your hands. I have written other books, but a book is like a child; you love all of them with each one being unique. This book is about my lifelong passion. Or at least it became my passion when I was sixteen years old. I was one of those kids who, when asked what I wanted to be when I grew up, always had the same answer. While some of my childhood friends wanted to be a firefighter one day and a doctor the next, I always had the same answer: I wanted to be a professional baseball player like my brother. It was my passion. Then a few months after my sixteenth birthday, I was hanging out at the beach with my friends. A complete stranger handed me a piece of paper with a photo of the ocean and a psalm written on it. For some reason, at that moment I moved from wanting to be a baseball player to wanting to spend my life helping teenagers.

Some people would say the little piece of paper was somehow a sign from God. Back then I wouldn't have said that. But I do think that my desire to help young people and their families was part of a calling on my life. I have never wanted to do anything else. Even when I speak at marriage conferences or write books for parents, my ultimate purpose is to help kids. We all know a secure marriage or a parenting plan will help kids in the long run.

I started working with teens right after that beach experience, and I never stopped. At the Burns family Christmas parties, my

Dad would invite me to sit at the "grown-up table" and I would turn him down! I loved teenagers, so I would always sit with them.

Because I have spent my entire adult life working in the world of teenagers and their families, I thought this book would be easy to write. Was I ever wrong! I have rewritten entire chapters, changed topics, moved around paragraphs, and struggled with what to say. Parenting teens is not easy, and what kids are going through today is tougher than in previous generations. I don't want this message to be depressing. At the same time, I want to be a realist. Because life is complicated for teens and for their parents, I don't want to give easy, trite answers to complex issues, but at the same time I want to create a very hopeful book.

As I began this project, I started brainstorming catchy titles. This book could have been called *I Hate You! Leave Me Alone! What's for Dinner?* or *How to Land the Helicopter Without Crashing* or *Who Is This Stranger in the House?* or a host of other corny titles. However, I settled on *Understanding Your Teen*, because I think it best describes the *felt need* of every parent with teens or preteens.

It's difficult to be a teenager today. Sure, the technological advances and opportunities are amazing, yet at the same time teens deal with pornography, terrorism, and so many experiences that were not around that day I felt called to work with teens. This is a unique generation: some are amazingly committed to making this world a better place and others are simply feeling lost and overwhelmed. It was interesting to hear the responses from adults when I told them I was writing a book on raising teenagers. I usually got a sigh, an eye-roll, and that far-off look that says, "I need this book!"

On a personal level, my wife, Cathy, and I thought that because of our background in youth ministry raising our own teens would be easy. It wasn't. We realized quickly that even though other kids might have thought we were cool, our own kids had other opinions! We are through the teen years and into "emerging adulthood" with our daughters now. I look back at their adolescence with both a fondness for the ride and the sobering knowledge that they could have made poor choices that would have lasted a lifetime.

So as you read this book, look for ways to incorporate some of the ideas into your parenting. Think of me as a friend who has already been through the teen years and is coming alongside you to help you navigate this season of life. The goal is to help you raise kids who love God and who will one day become responsible adults. I've also included reflection questions at the end of each chapter. It may be best to write down your answers and thoughts or to discuss them with your spouse or with a trusted friend.

One other note: throughout the book I describe teens interchangeably as her/him, she/he, and so on. I am using these words as generic terms for teens of either gender.

One thing I know about parenting teens is that you will be a much more effective parent if you stay calm, develop and follow a plan, and get as emotionally healthy as you possibly can. If you like roller coaster rides, then get ready for the ride of your life.

# PART ONE

# Parenting Teens to Become Responsible Adults

# 1

# *Understanding Your Teenager*

Youth is intoxication without wine.

**JOHANN WOLFGANG VON GOETHE**

I swear parents act like they
weren't teenagers before.

**ALLISON, AGE THIRTEEN**

**I**T SEEMS TO COME OUT OF NOWHERE, at least to the first-time parent of an adolescent. Yesterday your kid was just a kid. You have done a pretty good job raising him. After all, he's still alive, right? You've loved, sheltered, fed, clothed, protected, and taught him. It hasn't always been easy, but over the years, you came into your own as a parent. You hit your parenting stride! You know what to do (most of the time), when to do it, and how to do it. You've upheld your end of the parenting bargain. Bravo! But when the transition to adolescence strikes, it can come as quite a shock.

This morning you woke him up to get him going for school and he copped an attitude with you! You've never seen this before. Maybe he was just extra tired today? It could happen, right? Maybe this new attitude was just an aberration, a random pothole in the smooth road of family life. But then this afternoon when he came home, he didn't give you his customary kiss hello. He didn't even give you a hug. You got a grunt while he seemed preoccupied with texting his friends. He has always been affectionate toward you. But today he seemed downright surly instead, and then rushed to his room and closed his bedroom door. *What just happened?*

Welcome to the wacky and sometimes weird world of adolescence! Yes, change often occurs suddenly. You may have seen some initial signs of adolescence appearing here and there, but you ignored them as quirks. Now, over the course of a few days, weeks, or months, your precious, innocent child has disappeared. And you're not exactly sure who that stranger is living in your house! I thought that would never happen to my kids. My entire adult life had been dedicated to helping teenagers succeed and many of them actually thought I was cool. But when my own kids became teens, the last word they would have used to describe me was *cool*. I'm happy to report that they have now become responsible adults who actually think my wife and I are cool again. We survived, and so did our kids. But looking back, Cathy and I remember the emotional vertigo that the introduction of teenagers into our family dynamics caused.

If you are like my wife and I were when our kids were teens, you are trying to understand your teenager and are asking questions like: "What happened to my compliant little boy?" "Where did he get *that attitude*?" "Where is that *stink* in his bedroom coming from?" "And what exactly *is* that stink?" (Trust me on this one: you may *need* to know, but you don't always *want* to know.) I understand.

I've asked those questions and a lot of others about deeper and more complicated issues. You will find through these pages that you are not alone. Helping your child transition from childhood to adulthood is just not a simple task. Frankly, it's not easy for either the parent or the child.

I hope that this book will answer many of your questions. It's designed to tackle the key issues of the teen years. As we begin the journey of how to successfully parent teenagers, there is some important ground to cover first so that you can ultimately become the parent you long to be and the parent your teenager needs you to be. So buckle up your seat belt. You are in for a ride. The good news is that your precious child who morphed into the "stranger in the house" will one day soon become a responsible adult and may even give you the grandkids you desire.

## IT'S JUST A PHASE

Keep in mind that adolescence is a phase, a transition from childhood to adulthood. During a particularly rough time with one of my kids, I bought a blank card with a picture of an ocean and a palm tree on the front. I then wrote a quote by Maureen Hawkins that perfectly described my feelings about our daughter: "Before you were conceived I wanted you. Before you were born I loved you. Before you were a minute old I would have died for you. This is the miracle of life."

Somehow, the moment you have a child, part of your heart is ripped out of you and placed in the heart of your child, and you will never be the same. A late-night phone call while one of the kids is out always causes anxiety. A cough, a fever, or a sports injury brings panic and worry. A poor decision about morals and values causes terror in our souls. Raising teenagers is not for the weak at heart. Before we can help our kids become responsible adults, we have to understand a bit about these teenage years.

*Culture gives birth . . . to adolescence.* Parenting teenagers would be so much easier if we had hundreds of years of consistent wisdom from parents of teenagers to draw from, but we don't because adolescence as a recognized stage of life is a rather recent concept. Would you be surprised to learn that the word *teenager* was first introduced to the world in 1941 in, of all magazines, *Popular Science*? It's true! If world history was an elephant, adolescence wouldn't amount to much more than a mosquito sitting on the end of its trunk.

Until recently, there was *no* distinct life stage that we know today as adolescence. Most cultures only recognized two life stages: childhood and adulthood. A person was either in one stage or the other. At or about the age of puberty, children were simply deemed to be adults and were expected to take on full adult responsibilities. Sure, young "adults" then still faced the same human development tasks and processes that teenagers face today. But historically, the world presented them with much less freedom and much more responsibility. They were needed to contribute to the family economy and were kept busy in adult activities such as plowing fields, repairing barns, or tending to livestock. The average teenager would have had to figure out the big questions of life and find their place in the world while fully participating as adults.

But in the early- to mid-twentieth century, several large societal changes upset the status quo and led to the creation of adolescence as an identifiable phase of life. I won't bore you here by going into extensive detail about those changes. (You can google "the history of adolescence" if you're really interested.) What is critical to understand is that these changes created a new space where most teenagers no longer had to make the jump straight from childhood to adulthood. Because teens were not needed to help put food on the family table, and their role in the family became less clear, the relationship between teens and their parents became more complicated. Parents and teenagers alike were confronted with this new reality. Although no parent would want to go back to the direct jump from childhood to adulthood, we have to acknowledge that understanding adolescence is challenging. And just when we think we have figured teenagers out, they change.

Because teens were given much more freedom and much less responsibility than ever before, that raised a question: What would they do with all of their newfound freedom and time? Popular culture provided the answer. Savvy businesses perceived the emerging market for adolescents and got to work. My friend and teen culture expert Walt Mueller captures the essence of what happened in his book *The Space Between: A Parent's Guide to Teenage Development*, where he writes:

> Those who had something to sell segmented teenagers away from children and adults, creating a distinct youth culture that was targeted with food, clothing, cars, books, movies, and everything else imaginable—all of it made and marketed just for them. By the mid-1950s, teenagers even had their own music (hello, Elvis!) that spoke specifically to their interests and experience.[1]

Advances in technology and media (radio, telephone, TV, and magazines) made marketing goods and services to teenagers exponentially easier and more effective.

The marketers have never looked back. In the generations of teenagers that have followed, marketers have successfully shaped youth culture through engineering, re-engineering, and eventually recycling products and services that keep adolescents interested and buying.

In a real way, culture stole your precious, somewhat innocent child and made her into a stranger. And if these changes had not taken place, your teenager today might be a contributing and productive member of your family holding adult-like responsibilities, such as churning the butter, slopping the hogs, and milking your cows every day. And as crazy as it may seem, they would probably be giving you grandchildren instead of driving you crazy with their addiction to social media. Can you even imagine? Of course you can't, and for that matter, you don't want to.

*Adolescence itself is now an adolescent.* How society views adolescence has continued to evolve and change. Like a rebellious teenager, adolescence as a life phase has acted up and acted out. Not content to stay as it was, it grew over time, became moody, and refused to be pinned down. It seems that today adolescence is itself an adolescent.

Pinning down adolescence to a specific age range is simply impossible! Here's why: for the sake of discussion, let's define the range of adolescence as the period of life between the onset of puberty and adulthood. Let's keep everything simple by saying that adulthood is reached when a person reaches financial independence. Okay. So, when we were adolescents the range was somewhere around thirteen to around twenty, give or take a year or two. But now, both the onset of puberty and the point of financial independence have shifted. The average age of the onset of puberty has shifted younger while the age of economic independence has shifted older. The result is that the range of adolescence is now more like twelve to twenty-six, give or take a year or two. Yikes! This has huge implications for you: your kid will hit puberty sooner than you did and will stay an adolescent for longer than you did. (This means you can kiss that empty nest and early retirement goodbye!)

Although theories on the evolution of adolescence abound, the more helpful course for you is to focus on the way things *are* and what it means for you as the parent of a teenager.

## THE NEW EMERGING ADULTHOOD

Without a doubt, one of the biggest contemporary changes to the concept of adolescence has centered on the scientific and cultural recognition of "emerging adulthood."

In 2004, Dr. Jeffery Jensen Arnett published research in the book *Emerging Adulthood: The Winding Road from the Late Teens Through the Twenties.*[2] Arnett sees emerging adulthood as a period during the late teens and twenties where young people figure out who they are and what they want out of life. He makes the case that although emerging adulthood is a season full of challenges and anxiety, it is an important and healthy life phase that gives young people an extended time of self-focus that enables them to become comfortable with their identity, build skills, and identify their passions before committing to full adult responsibilities like career, marriage, and family. Essentially, emerging adulthood has effectively pushed back the age at which young people embrace full adult responsibilities.

Many experts have their opinions about emerging adulthood, but I'm not going to argue for or against it. I simply want you to be aware that the concept is already widely embraced in culture today. When Cathy and I sat at our youngest daughter's university graduation, the speaker announced to the students that a majority of them would, in the next few years, move back home and spend some time living with their parent or parents. There was an audible groan—not from the students but from the parents! All of our kids experienced seasons as twentysomethings of moving back in with us. It's not exactly how we drew up the game plan when our kids were in their teens, but in today's culture, it's common.

Surely you are aware of young people in their twenties who live at home with their parents or are pursuing graduate degrees or bounce around from one job to another or from one relationship to another or all of the above. Your kids *are* going to grow up with emerging adulthood as the recognized pathway to reach adulthood. And what you believe about emerging adulthood will influence how you parent your teenager. Depending on your approach to parenting your kids during their teenage years, they may still be living in your basement when they are twenty-nine years old. One of the key principles in this book is to parent your children to become responsible adults, even if that happens later than you imagined.

## CHANGE HAPPENS. CHANGE MATTERS.

Yes, we were all teenagers once upon a time. All of us have been thirteen, fifteen, and eighteen. But because so much has changed in our society and culture over the years, none of us experienced adolescence the same way our kids will, and certainly *none* of us know what it is like to be a teenager today. So, even though we were all teenagers once, we were never the age of today's teens. They experience so much at an earlier age than we did.

It can be helpful to remember what it was like to be a teenager because those memories serve to engender empathy and compassion for your teen. But your memories of how life used to be as a teenager must never create the foundation for how you parent your kids today. If, for example, you tell your daughter you think she should hang out at McDonald's more with her friends (after all, it's what you did when you were a teen), she'll likely give you the evil eye, pull out her smartphone, find a Google image of an old lady in a rocking chair, and post a meme on Instagram that reads, "I swear my mom was never a teenager."

If you are a member of Gen X, you were part of the latchkey kid generation. Perhaps you were one of the many children and teens who were left alone to fend for yourself much of the time. Your parents may have been nearby and accessible in theory, but we now know that many Gen X teens felt abandoned by their mom and dad. They often perceived their parents as too busy, too distracted, too focused on their own lives and careers, and as a result, they felt disconnected from them. Now, as a Gen X parent of a teenager, you may have swung the pendulum the other way. Sure, you're busy too. But you've likely made it a priority to spend more time with your kids and to pay more attention to them than your parents did. You are likely closer and more connected to them. These are awesome gifts that you are giving to your kids, and I applaud you for making these choices.

Yet it's important to be aware that how you parent your children will have downstream effects. Some "helicopter parents" attempt to avoid the mistakes of a previous generation. They are well-intentioned and invested in their kids' lives. But many of their children are *not* learning responsibility. Those that are over-parented find it difficult to transition to responsible adulthood. *Parents of this generation of teens need to land the helicopter so their kids will not be overly enabled.* The challenge is to successfully parent your teen without "over-parenting" them.

While your teenager may be unaware of the social and cultural forces influencing them that have been at work for decades, she has been greatly shaped by them. And these forces are ever evolving. So I commend you for your desire to better understand your teenager. Your teen will need to find her way to adulthood in the twenty-first century as a person shaped (to some extent) by twenty-first-century culture. The good news is that the powerful forces of the culture don't have to be the last word in shaping your child's life. Authorities tell us that the most influential force in a child's life is you, their parent.

Now that we've begun to better understand the stranger in your house, let's continue by figuring out what is making her, so . . . uhmmm . . . *strange.*

 **REFLECTION QUESTIONS**

1. Looking back, what was the best part of life as a teenager for you?

2. Looking back, what was your biggest challenge as a teenager?

3. What do you think are the biggest differences between being a teenager today and when you were a teenager?

4. Does it seem easier or harder to be a teenager today? Why?

5. Are you comfortable with how you were parented as a teenager? Why or why not? Which parenting methods or skills used by your parents will you replicate with your own teenagers? How do you envision parenting your teenager differently?

# 2

# Learning the Developmental Stages of Adolescence

> "But, Dad, I gotta be a nonconformist," the teenager said to his father. "How else can I be like all the other kids?"
>
> **LES PARROTT**

> Adults teach you to stand up for yourself and fight for what you believe in until what you believe in is different than what they believe in.
>
> **HOWARD, AGE SEVENTEEN**

*I*T WASN'T EASY FOR ME when my girls became teenagers. Our loving, affectionate, obedient girls suddenly copped attitudes, danced with danger, said and did outrageous things, and sometimes weren't very fun to be around. When I heard about or saw their antics, my usual response was, "Are you kidding me? What were they thinking? I can't believe they did that!" Most of the time it wasn't horrible stuff, but it floored me how they could be so dangerous, outlandish, or plain stupid at times and almost angelic at other times.

The behavior of my teens really affected my confidence as a parent. It was clear they didn't like me as much as they used to, and I found myself frustrated with them more often than not. I was the dad who came from another era—as far as my kids were concerned, I had grown up during the dinosaur age. They frequently teased me about my music, choice of movies, and clothing style, all totally out of step with their teenage reality.

I remember when I became "no longer cool" with each of my three daughters. Even though each circumstance was different, when they reached the age of twelve or so, there was a definite change in the parent-child relationship. There were moments when they were away from their friends when I still received a lot of affection, but for the most part, they took a huge leap away from Mom and Dad and toward their friends. These changes were temporary, but I didn't know that back then.

Everything seems to be in flux for teens. Their bodies are growing and changing in ways that surprise (if not shock) them. Their minds are changing, and their emotions seem to run wild at times. They are experiencing peer pressure and becoming aware of the opposite sex. In their saner moments even they wonder why they act the way they do and question whether they are normal. As a parent who wants to make the most of your influence to help your teenager become a responsible and fully functioning adult, it is critical that you understand what is happening to the stranger living in your house. Helping you enlarge your perspective and grow in compassion for your teen is the goal of this chapter.

At its simplest, adolescence is about teenagers becoming their own persons. This process is called *individuation*. Teens are making decisions and taking actions that will differentiate themselves from you, their parents. In order to become a responsible adult one day, healthy individuation is a must, so this is a positive development.

When children are young, they get their identities from being just like mommy or daddy. As teens, they don't want to be like their parents anymore. They want to be *themselves*. The individuation process includes a healthy dose of disengagement from family. It may become more difficult to get your daughter excited about going on family vacations or even to get her to eat dinner with the rest of the family. She may not want to be seen with you or show affection in public. You may notice her becoming more secretive as she intentionally begins hiding areas of her life that she wants to keep private.

For many parents, these teen behaviors feel like rejection. I understand. But these behaviors are normal and even healthy. So try not to take it personally and seek new ways to stay connected.

When it comes to the topsy-turvy and inconsistent thoughts, attitudes, and behaviors of an adolescent, you can start by partially blaming these on your teen's brain. Seriously, blame the brain. If your bright and mature teenager has sometimes made some really poor choices, it is partly because the brain is still under construction.

I realize this idea that your teen's brain is not fully developed might not be comforting when faced with irrational behavior, but it does help make sense of things like poor driving decisions, a seeming lack of ability to evaluate consequences, and the everyday drama and emotions of teen life. Even though the brain is not to blame for every dilemma, parents who take the time to learn about adolescent development have a better handle on what is going on with their cherished children.

The one word that describes the teen years best is *change*. Teen bodies might look adult bodies, but teen actions fall somewhere between child and adult. Let's look at those changes from a developmental standpoint.

## PHYSICAL CHANGE

Most teens desire to measure up to the cultural norm in terms of physical appearance. Their bodies are getting extreme makeovers, and many feel as if they are wearing a sign around their necks that reads "Caution: New Body Under Construction." Both young men and young women are extremely aware of the changes, but the girls seem to be more vocal about it. Hair is growing where once only skin lived. Sexual organs are growing, or not growing fast enough. Acne seems to feed on the teenage skin and often puts adolescents in an awkward-looking stage. Even muscles and bones are growing, sometimes at an uneven rate. Some kids become uncoordinated and others lethargic when their bodies grow six inches over the summer.

The physical changes come with awkwardness and comparison. With two teenaged girls, one might be wearing a training bra while the other already looks like a young adult. Some guys in their early teens have mustaches and hair on their chests and under their arms, while other guys are staring daily in the mirror waiting for something to grow. Both tend to be insecure and self-conscious.

Even if the words go unspoken, most kids are painfully aware of their changing appearance. They play the comparison game and always lose because they find others who have more desirable physical attributes. Our job as parents is never to tease them about their appearance but to reassure them that eventually they will catch up with everyone else—or everyone else will catch up with them. As much as possible, reinforce the truth that God has made them special and unique (see Psalm 139:13-18 and Ephesians 2:10).

## SOCIAL CHANGE

Many parents find themselves caught off guard by the social development and the power of friends in the teen years. What happened to the child that would rather cuddle with Mom and play with Dad more than anything else in the world? Now her innocent wonder and childlike simplicity is being transformed by a new view of the world seen through the eyes of her social environment.

Adolescence is a time when teens often move from a relatively safe environment in a neighborhood elementary school to a much larger and more impersonal middle school and high school. They start making important relationships outside of their families, and these relationships are much more confusing and complicated than in previous generations. When I was a teen, we had fairly well-defined social groups who influenced us. Our parents could keep pretty good track of who our friends were and how they were influencing us. Today, through the expanding reach of social media and smartphones, it is possible for a parent to have no idea who their child's best friends and greatest influencers are. As with teens in past generations, teens today say to their parents, "Everybody's doing it." It's our job as parents to figure out who "everybody" is and how they're influencing our kids. This task is more difficult today than it was before.

It's important to give your teens as much face-to-face unstructured socialization with their closest friends as you can. Kids tend to want to hang out with their closest group of friends in what I call "friendship clusters." My advice is to try to make your home the place your teen and his friends want to spend time. This comes with a bonus: it gives you great opportunities to get to know the peers in your teen's cluster of influence without becoming a snoop.

When our kids were teens, our home was Grand Central Station. We hosted Fellowship of Christian Athletes every week. The youth group from church came almost weekly in the summer. We even postponed buying a new couch for the living room until after our kids were finished with the teen years. Even if you can't share your home for youth group, you can volunteer to drive kids or chaperone to get to know your teen's friends. My oldest daughter, now a parent herself, recently overheard me telling someone that I always volunteered to drive so I could get a better understanding of who was influencing my kids. My daughter then said, "And Dad would try to sneakily turn the radio down so he could listen in on our conversations." Oops—busted!

## EMOTIONAL CHANGE

Adolescence comes with somewhat intense emotion. One dad said, "I felt like it happened over night—one day she was my sweet little girl and the next day she was a moody, morose, angry teenager." That father probably saw glimpses of his sweet little girl in the midst of her moodiness, and she will probably move back toward that sweetness as she gets older. Until then, anxiety, sadness, worry, anger, self-doubt, and fear can occur with ferocious intensity. The lows can often be very low and the highs can often be very high. There is just too much change going on within them to not intensely affect their emotions.

As teens begin to experience adultlike emotions for the first time in their lives, they aren't sure how to handle them. Their emotions can and will turn on a dime, and any teen can and often does experience the gamut of human emotions over the course of one afternoon. So be prepared to join your teenager on her emotional rollercoaster ride! Be as patient as you can with the stranger in your house. She is an emotional rookie, and it will take time for her to learn how to handle and manage her emotions. Much of this will be learned through trial and error.

On this rollercoaster of emotional ups and downs, you can be your teen's solid ground. My mom was my safe place. Although she didn't tell me very often that she loved me, I knew she was my greatest cheerleader and listener. Teens don't always want Mom and Dad to rescue them, and they definitely don't want a lecture. Listening to your children, especially through their emotional extremes, gives them the safe place they need. Parents, your presence matters in the midst of emotional change.

## INTELLECTUAL CHANGE

"Who am I?" This is the big question behind adolescence. Your teen may not be using that exact phrase but it is behind many of their thoughts and actions.

The intellectual changes during adolescence are at least as big as the physical changes, but because they happen internally they may go unnoticed. These are the years when kids move from concrete to abstract thinking. You can tell your elementary-aged child what to do most of the time, and you don't even have to explain yourself very much. "Because I told you so" is often a good enough response. Trying this approach with a teen who asks why and has gained the ability to think abstractly can lead to arguments and conflict.

Keep in mind that as teens' intellectual capacities grow and move from childlike to more adultlike, what used to seem black and white now seems gray. They are searching for answers to questions about life that they have never considered before. And they are reevaluating their opinions of you. Unfortunately, this change of opinion is seldom in a parent-affirming direction. When your children were younger, you could do little wrong. You were the most wonderful, smartest, and strongest person. But when your teens break through the barrier from childhood into adolescence, they'll realize that you never were all-powerful and all-knowing and that you are not perfect. As they begin to process the world in a more realistic way, they will start to see the brokenness of human nature. It will take time to learn how to process, manage, and deal with all of this new information.

At this stage, teens need more dialogue and less monologue from their parents. They need a safe place where they can exercise their expanding minds. They need to be heard. I'm not talking about discipline and boundaries. We'll get to that later. I'm talking about the key role parents play in helping their kids learn to think more maturely by creating a secure and affirming environment at home. This is one of the greatest steps in preparing them to make healthy decisions in the adult years.

## SPIRITUAL CHANGE

One of the main reasons I have focused on young people all my life is that adolescence is such an important spiritual time. Most people who make a commitment to Jesus Christ do so before age eighteen.[1] It's exciting to see teens explore their spirituality, but it's also a bit scary for us parents. As they move from concrete to abstract thinking, they begin to see spirituality and faith differently as well. They may say and do things that go against their parents' faith understandings. One of our daughters believed she had to disown our faith to eventually claim her own. Though that wasn't an easy time, today her faith looks quite similar to ours.

At this stage of faith development, teens may not want to go to church, or they might say things about God just to push your buttons. Your teen may move between passionate belief and passionate doubt. One morning your son or daughter may sincerely feel called to become a missionary to starving children, and later in the day he or she will tell you they don't believe in God anymore and want nothing to do with church. Both feelings are real, and both feelings are a normal part of faith development. This vacillating is part and parcel of teenage spirituality. Don't panic during your teen's season of searching. A majority of young people are on a spiritual quest, and we can't mistake skepticism or doubt as a sign that they are not interested.

Some parents respond to this spiritual searching by smothering their kids with their own faith. This rarely, if ever, provides the results that parents are looking to achieve. Sure, you can set boundaries ("As long as you live in our home, we expect you to attend church"), but don't spend much time preaching at them. Generally, lecturing and preaching at teenagers often results in pushing them further away from their parents' faith. Instead, give generous amounts of space to allow for and even to affirm their difficult faith questions.

When it comes to faith development, teens are experiential, so whenever possible, empower your teen to put her faith into action. During a tenuous time in the faith development of one of my daughters, we went on a mission trip together where we served and worked with poor children in Ecuador. Putting her faith into action caused my daughter to do some important thinking and soul searching, and one month after college graduation, she moved to Ecuador to invest a year of her life working with kids.

Here's the point: teens need regular occasions to act out their faith. We can't all go with our kids to a foreign country to do mission work, but we can help them find the time and the opportunity to do hands-on ministry and to learn that faith includes the call to serve.

Whether it be physical, emotional, intellectual, or spiritual change, think of adolescence as *transition*. Part of your job as a parent is to help your teen develop a sense of identity, establish healthy relationships, make wise decisions, and develop a relationship with God. They have to figure it out mostly on their own, but you can coach them if you understand why they act the way they do.

## MARK YOUR CALENDARS, BUT USE PENCIL

Once adolescence is underway, the race to adulthood begins. But in this race, think in terms of a marathon instead of a sprint. Teens mature in different stages and on different time frames. Each kid is unique. Still, there are some general patterns that are helpful to parents as they look ahead to the adolescent years. We can divide adolescent development into four stages. You will notice that in the following summary ages overlap since kids develop at different rates physically, socially, emotionally, intellectually, and spiritually. So mark your calendars, but use pencil so you can make changes as time goes by.

*Pre-adolescence* (ages nine to eleven). This is a time of preparation for adolescence. Kids are typically asking lots of questions, and you may notice the first physical changes taking place, particularly in girls.

*Early adolescence* (ages eleven to fourteen). Puberty has set in. This stage is characterized by lots of change and newness. Emotions are all over the place, and kids are searching for their identity.

*Mid-adolescence* (ages fourteen to eighteen). Experimentation is an important part of this period. These teens may be a bit cynical about authority, and they are often egocentric and self-absorbed. Friends are very influential. By the later part of this stage, you may begin to see the light of adulthood dawning and the beginning of healthy decision making.

*Late adolescence or emerging adulthood* (ages eighteen to mid-twenties). In earlier generations this was considered adulthood. Most people got married and even had children of their own. Today, not so much. In the last ten years, experts have coined the phrase "emerging adulthood" to describe a demographic of young people facing all kinds of complicated issues such as moral decisions, career paths, and financial considerations. These late adolescent issues are rarely resolved until the late-twenties.

Change is part of the teenage reality. Understanding these transitions helps you support your child as he or she grows toward responsible adulthood.

 **REFLECTION QUESTIONS**

1. How might learning about these adolescent developments affect your parenting methods with your teenager?

2. Of the adolescent developmental changes mentioned in this chapter, which is the most immediate and critical for your teenager to work through? Why?

3. What ideas do you have for helping your teenager deal with this challenge?

4. How comfortable are you handling your teenager's questions and doubts about faith? Explain.

5. What stage of adolescent development is your child in today (pre-adolescence, early adolescence, mid-adolescence, emerging adulthood)? How is this stage making an impact on your family?

# Shaping Behavior Without Crushing Character

He who is carried on another
man's back does not appreciate
how far the town is.

**—AFRICAN PROVERB**

Please pass me that
parenting handbook. I need
to smack my kid with it.

**—JORGE, FATHER OF TWO TEENAGE BOYS**

*S*HAUN CAME INTO MY OFFICE with his parents, but it was the last place he wanted to be. His mom and dad, on the other hand, were hoping that something good would come from our conversation. They were emotionally shattered. His mom was close to tears before she even started talking. Shaun's dad was quiet, pensive, and a bit removed. I sensed he had reached his limit with Shaun, and maybe with his wife too. Shaun's mom told me her life was in turmoil and that she didn't feel supported by her husband. Apparently he had taken a backseat when it came to discipline and setting boundaries with Shaun. For a moment I wondered if they needed marriage counseling more than advice about Shaun. Many couples who are raising teenagers today need a bit of both.

Shaun seemed to be a typical adolescent who was going through a somewhat extreme experimental phase. He was doing poorly at school, talking back to his parents, exhibiting a horrible attitude, and being generally disobedient and rude at home. As his mom talked about what was going on, Shaun slouched more and more. Of the three of them, Shaun was wearing the least stress on his countenance. The funny thing was, I sort of liked Shaun. I could tell he understood his parents' concerns, but was simply choosing to rebel. Yes, he was mixed up and being disobedient, but in my heart I felt he wasn't as bad as his mom claimed.

My guess, based on our conversation, was that Shaun had been indulged by overprotective parents. He was acting like an "entitlement king," and he wasn't going to get with the program until he felt some pain. Someone once told me, "When the pain of remaining the same is greater than the pain of changing, you will change." It's "the pain of discipline or the pain of regret" philosophy. Shaun hadn't felt much pain of regret at this point in his life, and he definitely wasn't as responsible as his parents had hoped he would be. He didn't have the internal motivation to improve, and the external motivation from his parents wasn't working.

Shaun's mom went on about his poor grades, poor attitude, poor friendships, and lack of desire for spiritual growth. She was clearly overwhelmed. I thought to myself, *Wow. This woman is carrying it all on her back.* She then went after her husband and his lack of leadership in the home. He got mad and defensive and said to me, "I *am* concerned about Shaun. He's wasting his potential, but she's acting crazy about it." Shaun nodded his head in agreement with his dad. I felt the mom's pain—my own three strong-willed teens didn't always walk the straight and narrow path. Shaun yearned for freedom. But it seemed like the more freedom he took, the poorer choices he made. Meanwhile, his mom was digging in her heels and wanted more control.

This tug of war between a teen's freedom and a parent's control is common. As kids move toward independence, this dance of freedom and control between teen and parent is anything but a graceful waltz. It often seems more like doing the chicken dance. Even in the healthiest of families, teenagers aren't ready for complete freedom. Even in the healthiest of homes, parents can struggle giving up their control. Yet little by little, parents *must* give up the control they exert over their teenager's life so the teen will eventually enjoy responsible adulthood.

By the time it was my turn to talk, our time was almost up. I was hopeful these relationships could be salvaged. But it would take responsible decision making not just from Shaun, but from his mom and dad as well. I turned toward the parents and was silent for about fifteen seconds to get their attention. The pause felt like a long time, but I wanted my words to count. "You are taking on all of Shaun's poor choices. You need to take that monkey off your back and place it squarely where it belongs—on his back."

## GET THE MONKEY OFF YOUR BACK

Micromanaging parents never get the results they hope for, and most often they end up disappointed. The most effective parents are those who surrender the control they really don't have and offer choices to their teens. That is the way to teach responsibility and respect.

The responsibilities of growing up shouldn't all rest on the shoulders of parents. We have to let our teens go and let them grow. The most valuable lessons in your teenager's life will often be learned as the result of the poor decisions he makes. Pain often comes before real freedom. If we as parents continue to indulge and enable our teenagers, we are helping to create irresponsible kids who are not going to grow up to become responsible adults.

One woman said, "Our son has everything. I just don't understand why his grades and behaviors are so bad." She was missing the point. Because she indulged her teenager, why on earth would he want to take on the responsibility needed to make better decisions?

The end goal in parenting is not to raise obedient kids but to raise responsible adults. To do that, you will need the incredible discipline of taking the monkey off your back and placing it on your teen's. Even in their failures you will be helping them build character without crushing their spirit.

## UNITED WE STAND, DIVIDED WE FALL

When it comes to discipline and boundaries, parents should try to stand united. When they are on the same page with discipline, boundaries, and consequences, they are halfway there. But it's not easy. Very few parents are naturally on the same page when it comes to discipline. Maybe it's dad who is too lenient and wants to befriend the teen and mom who has to do all the discipline. Maybe it's the opposite. But the kids take advantage of the divided front, and the parents end up resenting one another.

The easiest way to get on the same page is to keep the goal in front of you: to build your child's character and to help him or her become a responsible adult—not to make your child happy. Though it's sometimes difficult, the more united you can be and the less mixed messages you send to your kids, the better off they will be. Someone once said, "I don't know the secret of success for families, but I do know the secret of failure: trying to keep everybody happy all the time." That really does make a difference in our parenting.

Getting on the same page means developing a philosophy of parenting that both parents can agree to. Then work the plan, stay calm, and do what you can do to stay emotionally healthy. This can be difficult for a married couple, so divorced parents trying to co-parent their children often find being united in parenting even more difficult. It is still a worthy goal. Parents could read a book together once a year or go to a parenting seminar. Counseling or family coaching could also be helpful.[1]

It takes time, energy, and intentionality to get on the same page as your spouse, but it will strengthen your relationship and keep you from always parenting in reactive mode.

## LEAD WITH LOVE, PURPOSE, AND AUTHORITY

I fear that too many parents have indulged and enabled their children to such an extent that they have helped create irresponsible and even narcissistic ones. When we have weak, inconsistent discipline and poor boundaries, kids just aren't willing to grow up. I don't mean that kids shouldn't be nurtured and affirmed. Every child needs parents who can be irrationally positive toward them. But they also need us to express expectations, set high standards, and hold them accountable. In other words, our kids need us to lead.

What does leadership mean? I have spoken to and studied leaders in all fields of life. One thing they have in common is a consistent message. They model what they expect and they keep on task. With an excellent leader there is seldom a doubt about who is in charge. Parents are the leaders in their home. But the question in many homes of rebellious teenagers is "Who is really in charge?" This question must be settled, and the only healthy answer is that the parents must take the lead. Inconsistency or poor modeling will place your kids in the leadership position—that isn't healthy for anyone. So parents must eliminate any power struggle from the relationship and resolve authority issues. I tell people at our seminars, "Don't argue and don't fight with your kids." It is much more difficult to mentor and lead if you and your children are always fighting.

Cathy and I have a daughter who could win most of the arguments in our home. She is dynamic, articulate, and can argue either side of an issue. When she was a teenager she liked to argue for the sake of arguing, and she stretched the boundaries whenever possible. There were times she was just exhausting. Then one day, a therapist friend gave us two words of advice: "Quit arguing." If you think about it, people seldom argue with their leaders. We had to hold our ground.

Holding your ground can be wearisome, but it is always worth it (although you probably already know this from your own life experience). To help communicate with our kids about discipline-related issues, Cathy and I came up with the "Confident Parenting Talking Points." I wrote about them in greater detail in my book *Confident Parenting.*[2]

Learning to resist arguing with a teen who is pushing your buttons isn't easy, but there are three phrases I've found to be extremely helpful to diffuse potential arguments with teens:

1. "I feel your pain." If your teen knows your expectations and they break them, or if they suffer consequences from poor

decisions, let them know you care and that you feel their pain. You have empowered your teenager to make healthy decisions, but when she doesn't do that, you can show her empathy while holding her accountable. In a HomeWord parent podcast, John Rosemond shared what he told his own kids: "If I was your age, I'd feel the same way. The answer is still no, but you are doing a great job expressing yourself."

2. "Nevertheless." This might be the most important word in the English language to show who really is the leader in your home. Yes, we do feel their pain and we are listening; *nevertheless,* the consequences are going to stay. Adapting John's words to his kids, a parent might say, "I can understand how you feel, and I might have felt the same way when I was your age. *Nevertheless . . .*"

3. "Life isn't fair." The sooner your teen understands that life isn't fair, and that whining and complaining won't get him what he wants, he will quit trying to play the "make-it-fair" game. Whenever you can, let reality be the teacher for your kids. If whining and manipulating works for a teen even some of the time, it is the parent who has to live with the consequences. Here are more wise words from John Rosemond: "Parents should not agonize over what a child fails to do or does if the child is perfectly capable of agonizing over it himself."[3] Whatever your teen's age, it's about time he learns the truth that life isn't always fair, but it sure can be good.

## DEVELOPING CHARACTER AND RESPONSIBILITY

One of the ironies of parenting is that we have to give our kids freedom to fail in order for them to grow up. If you over-parent your teenager, your actions are shouting to her that you don't believe she can succeed by herself. We must go through the process of releasing control over our teens so they can move toward responsibility. A person who never learns to take full responsibility for their own life and actions will never have the chance to develop healthy character, or to be fully alive, and happy.

Foster Cline, in his excellent book, *Parenting Teens with Love and Logic*, offers four steps toward teaching your teens to become responsible.

- Step 1: Give your teen responsibility.
- Step 2: Trust that your child will carry it out.
- Step 3: When she does blow it, stand back and allow consequences to occur while expressing empathy.
- Step 4: Turn right back around and give her the same responsibility all over again because it sends a powerful implied message: "You're so smart that you can learn. People do learn from their mistakes and you're no different."[4]

The more parents can offer empathy for their kids' mistakes the better. For example, when grades are suffering, the appropriate response is something like this: "I hope you will be able to figure out how to pay the extra money for your car insurance until your good student discount kicks back in when you improve your grades." Part of teaching responsibility and character is holding your kids accountable for their actions. That's why it's important to express your expectations. The fewer surprises the better. Again, remember that often the most valuable lessons in life come from the consequences of making a mistake. Let reality be the teacher.

## EXPECTATIONS AND THE FAMILY CONTRACT

In some families a teen will live with clear expectations and consequences but still choose a path of unhealthy rebellion and misbehavior.

If healthy and consistent discipline isn't working, it's time to put together a family contract.

A family contract involves writing a plan with expectations and consequences for behavior. It is always best to create the contract together with your teen and never in the heat of the battle. When putting together a contract, keep it as simple as possible. Here is a simple outline to follow:

Issue

Expectations

Accountability

Positive Consequences

Negative Consequences

These five questions (and sample answers) can help:

1. What is the issue? (Lack of discipline with homework.)

2. What is a reasonable expectation? (Complete homework in a timely manner.)

3. How can we hold you accountable? (Daily homework check-in with one parent at an agreed-upon time.)

4. What are the rewards for a job well done? (a sense of accomplishment, feeling good about myself, college preparation, and perhaps buying a new outfit or celebrating with the family at a ball game)

5. What are the consequences if you do not meet the expectations? (unable to go to a four-year college right out of high school, poor grades, and costly car insurance as well as immediate consequences, such as no texting or social media until the homework is done, suspended driving privileges, or suspended sports activities)

Parents sometimes need a family contract. Shame-based parenting never works in the long haul. And preaching, criticizing, and yelling are never effective motivators—they will close your child's spirit toward you. With a contract, however, teens learn to discipline themselves and become more responsible.

## THE BOTTOM LINE

The bottom line in building character and responsibility is that there is hope. Even if you are in the pit of adolescent hormones, drama, and rebellion, know that most teens do make it through this stage and do just fine. Adolescence is a phase between childhood and adulthood. The truth to hold onto is that teens can be rude, selfish, and rebellious and still become responsible adults that one day you can laugh with about those transition years. Teens can make poor choices and experiment with poor behavior and still grow up okay.

Too many parents are emotional wrecks because they are carrying the weight of their children's behavior on their back. No matter how good of a parent you are, your child is quite capable of making poor choices and horrible decisions. Proper discipline does not guarantee proper behavior. However, if you develop and carry out a healthy parenting plan while getting as emotionally, spiritually, and physically healthy as possible yourself, you and your teen will have a much better chance of leading healthy, fulfilling lives.

 **REFLECTION QUESTIONS:**

1. What makes it so difficult to "take the monkey off your back and place it squarely on your teen's back"?

2. In what ways might you place more responsibility on your teen right now?

3. How would you rate your parenting leadership? If you find it lacking, what can you do to grow your leadership?

4. What are areas of character and responsibility that you will need to work on with your teen in order to help him or her develop into a responsible adult?

5. Do you need to develop a family contract? If so, how will you implement it?

# 4

# Energizing Your Teen's Spiritual Life

You can't really pass on to your children
something that you yourself don't have.
. . . If you are doing all you can to
stay close to God, your kids will
be much more likely to want
to do the same.

**WAYNE RICE**

God has no phone, but I talk to him.
He has no Facebook, but he is still my friend.
He does not have Twitter, but I still follow him.

**JARED, AGE FOURTEEN**

*I* **GREW UP IN THE SHADOWS OF DISNEYLAND.** When I was
a child, the incredible Matterhorn roller coaster was my favorite—
I never tired of riding it. Recently, my wife and I had a hot date
to Disneyland after several years away. The very first ride she

wanted to go on was the Matterhorn. It brought back great memories, but halfway through the ride I thought I was going to vomit! I found out I like calmer, gentler rides these days, the kind that don't make my insides feel like they are churning all around.

The spiritual life of most teenagers is much more like a rollercoaster than a calm, gentle ride. As teens move from dependence toward independence, they naturally begin to explore and even question their spiritual belief system. I have talked to hundreds of teens who seem fully committed to God one day and doubt his existence the next. At camps or retreats they decide to become missionaries overseas, and a day later they are found smoking in the wilderness or making out with someone they just met.

The experimental phase of adolescence doesn't just affect moral behaviors like drinking and sexual promiscuity. It is also a major factor in developing a solid faith. As teens sort out their own beliefs, it can get pretty rough for parents who desire to pass on their faith. A teenager's faith is often contradictory and self-centered. What teenager hasn't asked God to give him a better grade on a test because he didn't have time to study? Or blamed God for not helping her get a date for the prom? The teen years can be filled with declarations: "I don't want to go to church anymore. It's boring and irrelevant." But these years can also be an intense time of spiritual formation. It was during my teen years that I was called to lifelong ministry. Even so, that didn't stop me from drawing outside the lines with my beliefs and behaviors.

As if on a rollercoaster ride, parents of teens must tighten their seatbelts and hold on for dear life. At the same time, with an informed understanding of how faith develops, you'll be better prepared for the ride, and you might even find yourself enjoying it along the way.

## FAITH DEVELOPMENT AND TEENS

As kids move beyond a more childlike, concrete way of thinking to more adultlike, abstract patterns of thought, it is not uncommon for them to struggle with their faith. That is what happened with TJ. One day he told his parents he didn't want to go to church anymore. He said he didn't believe in God like he used to and he thought church was boring and irrelevant. His mom and dad didn't know what to do: Should they force him to go to church? Should they try to engage his newfound skepticism?

I asked if I could meet with TJ. It was clear that he was a bit unmotivated in life (not unusual for a teenager) but that he respected his parents and wasn't antagonistic. All in all, he seemed like a good kid. I looked for deeper issues, such as immoral behaviors, broken relationships with parents, abuse, or anything else that might lead to his negative feelings about his faith. But I didn't find anything. His main struggle was understanding how a loving God could allow death, war, poverty, and abuse in the world. My response seemed to surprise him.

"I think your questioning is healthy."

"Really?"

"Yes. You're asking great questions for someone your age," I told him. "I've had many of those same questions, and sometimes they creep back into my mind."

"My parents think there's something wrong with me."

I replied, "The only thing wrong would be if you quit searching for the answers to these really important questions." I then added, "I do wonder if your perception of the church as irrelevant is more about your attitude than the church because I know several people who really enjoy your church." He smiled but said nothing.

I then offered TJ a fifty-day challenge. "How about investing five minutes a day for the next fifty days in your spiritual quest and we'll meet with every two weeks to talk?" I handed him my devotional book *Addicted to God*,[1] and he took my challenge. By the time we met next, he had gone back to church and had even had some dialogue with his parents about faith. Today, TJ is an adult with a strong and energized faith.

As parents, we must remember that just because teenagers seem bored with their faith doesn't mean they hate God. TJ was actually going through a healthy process of disowning his parents' faith in order to develop a faith of his own. The questions and convictions were all part of growing up spiritually. In fact, it would probably be wise for churches to teach parents more about faith development and spiritual formation. Let me explain.

James Fowler, a pioneer in the field of faith development, identified six stages of faith.[2] At stage one, children simply take on the faith of their parents. It's a simple faith, and mainly they mimic their parents' attitudes and even their prayers. At stage two, children start to connect faith to their church community and extended family, but it is still close to their parents' belief system. At stage three, kids' faith is not personalized as much as we think, but they are taking on the faith of their church or denomination. Stage four, what Fowler called the "individual stage," is when children's faith becomes their own. Sometimes they even move outside the faith of those closest to them. At this stage, faith is usually a bit simplistic and yet a serious commitment. Stage five is when adolescents begin to embrace some of the paradoxes of their faith. They are not shattered by unanswered prayer or the suffering in the world. Their faith is actually healthy, but a bit more complicated. The last stage, stage six, involves a more complex state of faith that often doesn't solidify until adulthood. In this stage, people develop their sense of mission and calling in life.

By being aware of the normal stages of faith in a teenager's spiritual formation, I hope you can relax a bit when she expresses doubts and questions. This isn't the time for parents to preach or condemn, but rather a time of opportunity to explore the issues in question, to continue setting a solid example for authentic faith, to help teens connect their faith to the adventure of everyday life, and to take advantage of teachable moments along the way. Let's turn our focus to the key aspects of successfully passing on your faith and energizing your teen's faith.

## ENERGIZING YOUR FAMILY'S SPIRITUAL LIFE: SET THE PACE

Mark Holmen, a family ministry expert, tells a story about his days as a youth worker. He gave the students in his church a questionnaire to fill out in order to establish how much his ministry had influenced their faith. He laughingly admits that he thought it might help him get a raise. But the results weren't what Mark expected. By far the greatest influence was moms, followed by dads, grandparents, other relatives, siblings, friends, and finally, the church. Similar conclusions have been found in more formal studies. This is not to downplay the important role youth ministry and your local church can play but rather to remind us that as parents we set the spiritual pace for our kids, for good or bad.[3]

Christian Smith's *Soul Searching is* based on the conclusions from the landmark National Study on Youth and Religion. Smith states: "Most teenagers and their parents may not realize it, but a lot of research in the sociology of religion suggests that the most important social influence in shaping young people's religious lives is the religious life modeled and taught by their parents."[4] When you think about it, it makes sense. Teens with parents who attend church regularly will also be inclined to attend church regularly. With a healthy faith modeled at home, kids will naturally develop more of a faith mindset.

The good news is that we do not need to be perfect parents. Teens today are looking for authenticity more than anything else, and it is possible to model a life of integrity even in the midst of developing your own spiritual life. When the Bible says, "Whoever walks in integrity walks securely" (Proverbs 10:9), the assumption is that if you live your life with integrity, not only will you have a more secure life but so will your children. According to researcher George Barna, parents are beginning to understand that they have the primary responsibility for teaching their children spiritual values. Barna found that 85 percent of parents believe they have the primary task of teaching their children about spiritual matters. But he also found that the majority of parents do not spend any time during a typical week discussing spiritual issues with their children. This disconnect is alarming yet understandable. It's difficult to take the time to lead our kids in spiritual principles when we are either too busy or too distracted.

In an excellent book on spiritual legacy, *Generation to Generation*, Wayne Rice says, "Busyness also keeps a lot of parents from being the spiritual leaders of their families. That's why the job so often gets outsourced to the church."[5] It is alarming how many well-intentioned parents will pour decades of intense effort into developing their children's ability to play soccer, do gymnastics, or play a musical instrument and yet completely ignore their spiritual development. Obviously it's complicated, and there are other reasons besides being too busy, but the point remains: *the primary task of spiritual training comes at home, with the church having the important role of coming alongside the family, not replacing the family.*

The biblical method of transmitting faith to the next generation is quite clear. Found in Deuteronomy 6:4-9, the Shema is still the most often-quoted Scripture. Recited every morning and evening in Orthodox Jewish homes, it is also the standard for our Christian faith:

> Hear, O Israel: The LORD, our God, the LORD is one. Love the LORD your God with all your heart and with all your soul and with all your strength. These commandments that I give you today are to be on your hearts. Impress them on your children. Talk about them when you sit at home and when you walk along the road, when you lie down and when you get up. Tie them as symbols on your hands and bind them on your foreheads. Write them on the doorframes of your houses and on your gates.

Notice that the Shema teaches three key elements of faith: loyalty to God, transmission of your faith to your children, and how you should daily share your faith with your family. The key to transmitting your faith is found in verse six: "These commandments that I give you today are to be upon your hearts." Then, only after you nurture your own loyalty to God can you "impress them on your children."

Excitement for God and his Word is caught, not just taught. Children see, children do. If our teenagers watch us cut corners and compromise integrity repeatedly, why wouldn't they do the same? If our teens watch us pursuing our own faith development with authenticity, they will most likely want to follow in our footsteps. When our daughter Christy was young, she was sitting in our living room reading a devotional book. When I asked her what she was doing,

she smiled and said, "I'm pretending I'm Mommy." Why? She had
seen Cathy sit in that same place day after day reading her devotional.

## ENGAGE IN FAMILY FAITH CONVERSATIONS

One of the difficult recent findings about teens and faith is that a
majority of teens who graduate from high school do not attend
church the following year. However, the research shows that kids
who grow up having healthy faith conversations at home are much
more likely to stay in church after the teen years, practice their
faith, and marry someone with similar faith values.

What is a faith conversation? Just talking about faith in a
helpful, positive, interactive manner. As parents, we always want
to be looking for those teachable moments and opportunities for
spontaneous interactions.

Many families introduce a weekly time of faith conversations to
their schedule. Our own family time included about twenty
minutes of faith conversation followed by prayer and chocolate or
other treats. (Who says you can't eat sweets and laugh together
while you are having faith conversations?) We used short Bible
studies borrowed from youth ministry, YouTube inspirational
videos, our own discussion starters developed from hot topics. One
discussion starter came right out of the Denver Post:

> As far as Regina Hammond is concerned, luck has little to do
> with it. The 37-year old flight attendant won $100,000 in a
> Colorado Lottery game on top of the $50,000 she won the
> previous year the same way. And she's not finished yet. Her
> goal is the multi-million grand prize. Hammond believes that
> prayer has paved her way to riches. "I pray to God to help me
> and He answers."[6]

Our family discussion centered on three options for thinking about the situation: God did answer her prayer, God didn't answer her prayer, or I'm just not sure. All of our family voted that we weren't sure. We then talked about the fact that sometimes God says yes to our prayers, sometimes no, and sometimes wait. We looked at what the Bible says about prayer. We talked about the lottery. It was a stimulating conversation, and my kids barely realized that in the process we were learning about prayer.

## PASS IT ON: RITES OF PASSAGE

Another way to pass along faith in your family is to incorporate it into celebrations of your children's important milestones with intentionality. This might mean celebrating a driver's license or a high school graduation, or even having a womanhood or manhood ceremony when your child is in the twelfth grade. In our book *Pass It On*,[7] Jeremy Lee and I encourage families to have an informal ceremony, give your child a symbol, and include significant others to celebrate the rite of passage.

Our family celebrates birthdays in a big way. At the end of a nice meal, each family member offers three words of affirmation to the one whose birthday it is. It's our way to celebrate another milestone.

## PRACTICE SPIRITUAL DISCIPLINES

I've always been intrigued by the advice Paul gave to his protégé Timothy: "Discipline yourself for the purpose of godliness" (1 Timothy 4:7 NASB). Another Bible version states the advice this way, "Train yourself to be godly" (NIV). Teaching our teenagers spiritual disciplines—in a sense training them to honor God—is something that can be done if we are proactive about it. It was Henri Nouwen who said, "A spiritual life without discipline is impossible. Discipline is the other side of discipleship."[8] Somehow the fine line between training and discipline is teaching our teenagers to love God out of a response for what he has done for them and not just because they feel some sense of family responsibility.

Some time ago I was speaking at a Christian school on prayer and devotional life. I challenged the students to spend five to ten minutes a day with God for the next fifty days. I even offered to take anyone who completed my "50 Day Challenge" out to lunch. Well, the students took me up on the challenge. The "50 Day Challenge" cost me $750 because so many kids followed through. At lunch, I asked them how the challenge affected them. Interestingly enough, fifty days was long enough to become a habit, and not a single teen told me it was not worth their time.

## HELP MAKE FAITH AN ADVENTURE

Jim Rayburn, the founder of Young Life, was fond of saying, "It's a sin to bore a kid with the gospel." As a family, it's important to periodically provide experiences that remind our kids that faith is an adventure. What we don't want is for kids to see faith as old fashioned, dry, or boring. Teenagers need to know that faith is relevant and practical and sometimes even a bit dangerous. When my two oldest daughters became teenagers, I took them to Mexico to do mission work. We worked hard building a church. The dirt and sweat and calluses on our hands were not what any of us were used to. I kept wondering if they were having an okay time. But years later one daughter served as a missionary for a year in South America, and the other one teaches in the inner city. Both point back to the Mexico mission experience as part of their faith journey to move them toward helping others.

Every family can find ways to have faith adventures, and every family can serve the poor and oppressed. I am always amazed how well teenagers do when they are challenged to move beyond their comfort levels and to make a difference in the lives of others. Even the most self-centered teenagers are inclined to move beyond themselves and to having their heart break with what breaks the heart of God. When this happens, growth occurs.

## PROVIDE EXPOSURE TO OTHER ROLE MODELS OF FAITH

You don't have to carry all the weight of modeling faith on your own shoulders. Yes, you are your teenager's primary faith influencer, but others can play a positive role as well. Make sure you provide your kids with plenty of opportunities to rub shoulders with other Christ-followers you know who will provide rich examples of integrity, authenticity, and faith. Surrounding them with these great people, friends, and mentors sends a clear message that people of faith aren't only found in your home or within the walls of your church. By "teaming up" your influence as a parent with other trusted role models, you are setting the table for a lasting legacy of faith that will serve your teenager through his or her lifetime.

That's why it is important to encourage your kids to be involved in your church's youth ministry program. Especially during the adolescent years, they need other role models besides you to be influencing them. We know that parents are the primary influencers in the long run, but there is nothing like another adult who influences our kids as well.

If for any reason you feel discouraged about your son's or daughter's faith journey, just remember that ultimately God is in control and his unfailing love is more powerful and eternal than even our love for our kids. Ultimately, it's a matter of putting our trust in the creator, sustainer and redeemer of life: Jesus. Our job is to put the words of Proverbs 3:5-6 into practice:

> Trust in and rely confidently on the LORD with all your heart and do not rely on our own insight or understanding. In all your ways know and acknowledge and recognize Him, and He will make your paths straight and smooth. (Amplified Version)

 **REFLECTION QUESTIONS**

1. What was your spiritual journey like when you were a teenager? How might your spiritual journey during adolescence inform your understanding of what your teenager is going through?

2. What kind of influence did your parents have—for better or for worse—on the development of your faith when you were a teenager?

3. Teens say that moms influence their faith more than dads. Why do you think this is so? How might dads increase their influence?

4. Does a teenage time of questioning and doubt make you uncomfortable? Why or why not?

5. What aspects of your faith would you like to pass along to your teenager? How would you like your teenager's faith to differ from your own?

# 5

# Creating a Media-Safe Home

Mom: What does IDK, LY, and TTYL mean?
Son: I don't know, love you, talk to you later.
Mom: OK. I will ask your sister.
Son: What?

**AWKWARD PARENT TEXT**

I refuse to open Snapchat
videos in public because I do
not trust my friends at all.

**TEENAGER'S POST FROM TUMBLR**

*N*O PARENT HAS EVER THOUGHT the world was perfectly
safe for his or her children. We taught our kids when they were
young to look both ways before they cross the street and not to
talk with strangers. We monitored the types of media they would
engage—or at least we tried to keep up. However, in today's world
it's *impossible* for parents to have complete control over everything

that is being sent to the eyes, minds, and brains of teenagers. So much of this generation's life is centered around media, and it is tempting them in every way.

Just recently the speaker at a conference in Louisiana asked all the high school guys, "How many of you have *not* seen pornography?" Not one guy raised his hand. They had all viewed pornography at least once.

Pornography, YouTube videos, TV shows and movies, video games, and everything on the Internet all has an influence on teens today, and much of it is not good. If anything is going to take down this generation of teenagers, it's going to be poor media choices. Most parents feel lost. Some feel hopeless.

One reason many of us feel helpless and even paralyzed by our kids' use of media is the learning curve media requires. Some of us have a hard enough time figuring out how to use our television remotes, and need our kids to help us change the channel. But we can't afford to bury our heads in the sand when it comes to technology. We must become students of our culture and see how media is influencing our teenagers. There is hope for those who persevere and try to create a media-safe home. At one time the "keep your kids in the bubble" approach might have worked, but it won't work today unless you move to a remote island.

HomeWord provides Christian parenting seminars on topics ranging from "Understanding Your Teenager" and "Confident Parenting" to "Teaching Your Children Healthy Sexuality." When it's time for Q & A, most of the questions are focused on media: "Should I allow my kids to have Snapchat?" "How many hours a day should I let my kids play video games?" "What types of music should I let my daughter listen to?" "Is it okay to let my son take his phone to bed with him at night?" The list goes on and on. The specifics of the parents' questions change as technology evolves, but the substance is always the same.

There is a story in the Bible about Joshua and Caleb and ten others sneaking into the Promised Land to scout it out and report back to Moses (Numbers 13). When they returned, they all agreed that the land was "flowing with milk and honey." There were wonderful fruits and beautiful streams. The land was good. But there was one problem—it was inhabited by powerful giants. Ten scouts, the majority, advised Moses not to enter the Promised Land. "The land is beautiful with bountiful food, but giants live in the land," they said. When it came time for Joshua and Caleb to make their report, they said, "We agree. The land is wonderful and the people are like giants." But they added, "Let us immediately go into the land, for God will give us victory." Both groups saw the same things in the Promised Land. But while the first group was paralyzed by fear, Joshua and Caleb believed that with God's help they could inhabit the land. Moses went with the minority report.

My point is simple. As we look at the giant of media that is influencing the minds and lives of our teenagers, we can either be paralyzed with fear or proactively take it on. Since we can't actually slay this giant or keep our kids from all media, we need a stealthier plan of attack. We will have to teach our teens to make wise and discerning decisions about what influences them.

## TECHNOLOGY IS NEUTRAL, MEDIA IS NOT

For better or for worse, we all use technology. For many, technology has become a partner in life, keeping us in touch with the ones we love, reminding us when to take medications, telling us how many steps we've walked today, and recommending a new restaurant for our next date night with our spouse. We love our phones, tablets, and laptops, even if we don't know much about most of the apps on them. In my own work, social media has been a big help with communication and engagement between HomeWord and the families, ministry leaders, and churches we serve. Today we have multiple websites, along with pages and profiles on Facebook, Twitter, Instagram, and Pinterest. We could not effectively interact with the same numbers of people we do these days were it not for technology. And yet, just as HomeWord uses technology and media for good, there are others vying for our teens' attention who use media for negative influence. The same cell phone your child is using can save a life or feed an addiction. Your teen can receive an encouraging message in the form of a text and receive a sext a minute later.

Parents don't need to become technology experts, but we do need to be aware of what's out there and how our kids are using the latest technology. I've had parents tell me, "I'm too busy to keep up with all the media my kids handle in a day." Yes, it can be overwhelming, but there is no excuse good enough to remain ignorant or in denial. When you had your child, God trusted you with the responsibility of protecting him or her. While this becomes more difficult as your kid reaches the teen years, as he or she experiences more independence and freedom, every teenager deserves their parent's best.

## LISTEN, READ, AND WATCH

The easiest way to stay on top of media that is influencing your teenager is to listen to what they listen to, read what they read, and watch what they watch. Yes, this means you have the right and responsibility to help choose what kind of music enters your home. Watching popular movies, YouTube videos, and TV programs will give you more insights than you may want. You should also become aware of social media apps and sites that are popular with teens, as well as video games, and other websites your kids tend to hang out on.

The best people to teach you about the influence of media are the teenagers closest to you: your kids and your kids' friends. I recommend that you make a list of various media you want to talk about with your kids, and then look for opportunities to ask and learn. Things worth considering as you seek to learn: How does this media influence my teen (positively, negatively, or neutrally)? How much time does my teen spend with this type of media each day? Each week? And what are the potential dangers of this type of media?

Here is a list of media you should become aware of:[1]

- Social media sites and apps (Instagram, YouTube, Snapchat, Twitter, Tumblr, Facebook, Pinterest, and Google+)

- Texting and messaging apps (WhatsApp, Kik, and Facebook Messenger)

- Video chat apps (Skype, Oovoo, and FaceTime)

- Live streaming apps (YouNow, Periscope, Meerkat, Livestream, YouTube Connect, and Facebook Live Video)

- Ephemeral apps (Snapchat, Xpire, Frankly, and Phantom)

- Videos (from old-fashioned DVDs to streaming video)

- Music and music videos

- Video game playthrough videos

- Chat and forums

- Blogs

- TV (broadcast and cable/satellite)

Space does not allow for me to comment on all of these categories, so you'll need to do some homework on your own. For now, here are some thoughts about a few of today's key media types that your kids will routinely be exposed to and influenced by.

*Smartphones.* Smartphones have become the primary delivery system of media to our teenagers. It wasn't that long ago when cell phones were only that—phones. Today, perhaps the smartphone feature used least today by teenagers is the phone itself! Teens prefer to use a smartphone's other modes of communication, and for them, texting and messaging apps are the most popular. In fact, if you call your teenager, it's likely she won't answer, but she will immediately reply to your text. Today's smartphone is much more than a phone; it's a pocket-sized supercomputer that connects to the world.[2]

This generation of teenagers has never known a world without the Internet. They have no memory of using a hardwired phone line to connect to it, or of dial-up modems and their noisy connection protocols. When they have a question about sex, they search Google. When they're writing a history paper and need to find the dates of the French Revolution, they ask Siri. While their smartphones cannot actually feed them, teens use their phones to order their pizza, pay for it, and arrange to have it delivered directly to wherever they are. Nine in ten teenagers go online from their smartphones, and of those who do, 94 percent go online daily or more often.[3]

Obviously, there are both benefits and dangers to your teenager's smartphone use. Make sure you have a written understanding of expectations with smartphone use and your kid's lifestyle.

*Visual media: movies, online videos, streaming providers, TV.* Visual media remains extremely popular with teenagers today, as it has been with previous generations of teens. The difference is that today, adolescents have a far broader range of video content to watch with virtually instant access to it from their smartphone or tablet. While TV is still a popular medium for visual media among teens, in recent years it has been surpassed by streaming video sources such as YouTube and Netflix and videos posted on social media outlets.[4] From an entertainment perspective, you may have no desire to do it, but I recommend that you periodically watch movies that are popular with teens to better understand what your kids are watching. Beyond this, periodically, invest some time to watch YouTube videos, Netflix or Google original programming, and TV shows that are popular with your kids or with teenagers in general.[5]

These days, pictures are amazingly popular with teens (think selfies), and while you may not consider photos as visual media, you should. If you have friended your teen on Instagram, Facebook, or other social media outlets (I hope that you will do this, although your teen may not appreciate it), you can browse through the many photos that will appear on these pages. A picture can be worth a thousand words when it comes to learning about media and its potential influence on your teen. I also strongly recommend that you don't add comments to your teenager's social media outlets. Far too many parents have either embarrassed their kids or gotten involved in a conversation they were not invited to join. It's best to be their silent friend. If you must comment, do it in person.

*Social media.* The culture changes so quickly. Does anyone still remember Myspace? There was a time when Facebook was the social media of choice for teens, but then their parents started using it, so they rapidly migrated to Instagram. Now Snapchat has become the most popular social media for teenagers. What's next? Wait until next year to find out.

Social media meets the adolescent's need for unstructured socialization with peers. So part of the job for every parent is to help teach their teen to discern just how social media affects our lives. Today, about eight in ten teenagers ages thirteen to seventeen use social media.[6] Social media scratches the adolescent's itch for social connection with their peers. They enjoy connecting and interacting with friends, making new friends, and sharing their thoughts and feelings through their social media posts. Social media weaves its way through and intersects with all other media types. So your teen is interacting with others using a combination of visual, audio, and textual media in their posts.

Selfies are huge in social media today largely because they are a perfect fit for teenagers in the throes of adolescent development, particularly as they work through the issues of identity, self-image, and self-esteem. Each selfie posted gives a kid the opportunity to test-drive her sense of identity and receive almost immediate feedback through social media. This feedback presents a double-edged sword, with positive and negative outcomes. As kids view feedback from selfies, they refine their awareness of identity, popularity, and fame, for better or worse.

Adolescent experts and parents alike suggest that ephemeral apps (apps where the posts are deleted after a period of time) such as Snapchat are potentially dangerous for teenagers—for all of the right reasons: kids can use them to send a sext, or other inappropriate pictures or video, with a false sense of security that no one but the recipient will *ever* see the images. Ephemeral apps are becoming the biggest form of bullying with teens. But tech-savvy kids can take a screenshot before the image disappears and then redistribute it, where it might reside in cyberspace forever.

One final thought about social media: as teens use it as a means to develop social skills, remember that because adolescence is a season of experimentation, they are likely to experiment. The online environment emboldens kids to communicate in ways they would not when in face-to-face conversation, or to engage in behaviors they typically would not. Highly sexualized comments, criticisms, rants, bullying, sexting, and creating profiles with an alternative identity, may all fall under the umbrella of social media experimentation. Again, parents cannot keep their heads in the sand with media; it's just too easy for your kids to stray.

*Music.* Listen to the music popular with your teenager and her friends. Favorite music styles include rap and hip-hop, indie rock, folk, electronica, Latin, country, and many more. Whatever the style, music continues to be a strong influence in the lives of teenagers, meeting three basic needs:

1. Musicians spend huge amounts of time communicating with young people (largely via social media)—providing *companionship.*

2. Musicians accept young people as they are—providing *acceptance.*

3. Musicians often relate to teenagers' problems through song lyrics—providing *identification.*

A parent must do the investigative work to know who and what is influencing their kids as well as help kids learn to discern how they are being influenced.

*Video gaming.* It's possible that your teen doesn't play video games, but it's not likely. A 2014 study by Northeastern University found that just 11 percent of US teenagers are not gamers. Modes of gaming have grown increasingly diverse. Games can be played almost anywhere, anytime on smartphones, tablets, laptops, computers, gaming consoles, and smart televisions. Online, games can be joined by players around the world.

Even if your teen is not playing games that are violent or sexual in nature, too much gaming can have a negative effect on your teen.

In fact, some experts believe that kids who play action games on a regular basis may undergo brain changes.[7] It is important to monitor the amount of time your teen spends playing games and to know what games he or she is playing. It's actually not a bad idea to play video games with your teen to the extent they will allow you to play.

## THE PARENT'S ROLE

Perhaps the two most prevalent approaches parents take with their teens regarding media use simply don't work: ignoring the dangers and being too strict.

Some parents put their heads in the sand when it comes to their kids' media use. It takes a lot of work for parents to help teens evaluate media, and they are going to push back on your opinions. It's easy for a parent to get worn down and give up. The other approach is trying to keep your teens in a bubble with too-tight restrictions. It might work during a child's younger years, but with teens, in general, boundaries that are too tight will cause them to rebel so much that they may run in the other direction.

So what's the right approach? Here's my best advice for parents.

1. ***Be a student of today's media.*** Remember what I said in the last chapter about the value and importance of becoming students of the culture. Start examining media through the following evaluation filters:

   - *Evaluate everything you see and hear.* This takes a lot of work, but it's worth it. When you evaluate, don't just position yourself as the bad cop. Tell your kids what you like and don't like and why, and help them to discern what they are putting into their minds. I had an odd feeling about a music group one of my daughters wanted to listen to, so I did my homework. Some in the band were married but clearly had no problem carrying on extramarital affairs. Another band member had been arrested for child pornography and having sex with a minor. So, I brought these issues to my daughter's attention. "So what do you think?" I asked. "They're gross," she responded. "I'm not going to listen to them anymore." Okay, so she never thanked me for my investigative skills, but she made the decision not listen to the group anymore and I didn't have to pull the plug.

● *Examine your own behavior.* Too many parents want their children to view healthy images, listen to clean music, and watch cute animal videos on YouTube, but aren't willing to discipline their own lives. If Dad watches raunchy movies and Mom reads *Cosmopolitan*, we should expect their teenagers to want to do the same. If Dad comes home from work and jumps on the computer for hours, his teens won't understand why they can't. Keep this verse in mind: "'Everything is permissible for me,' but not everything is beneficial. 'Everything is permissible for me,' but I will not be mastered by anything" (1 Corinthians 6:12 CSB).

2. *Establish media boundaries and consistent consequences.* Families should set boundaries and time limits for TV, smartphones, social media, laptop/computer use, video gaming, texting, and any other media use. It's ultimately up to you to set and enforce those boundaries, but they will be most effective when you and your teen create them together. I suggest that you and your teen work together to come to an agreement on what is and what is not acceptable in your home.[8] Remember, people support what they help to create. These boundaries

should change as your kids move from pre-adolescence to emerging adulthood, but at every age, they need your direction and guidance to help stay within healthy boundaries.

- *Keep technology and digital devices out of your teen's bedroom at night.* This should be a no-brainer for parents, but many teens have unlimited online access through their smartphones, tablets, and laptops while in the privacy of their bedrooms. If your teen has hours of unsupervised access to any and all types of media, you are asking for trouble. Move digital devices to more public areas in the home. With today's smartphones, there is no way to absolutely guarantee that your teen won't view inappropriate media when he is sitting across the living room from you, but it is less likely there than if he is in his bedroom.

  My friend and colleague at Azusa Pacific University, Dr. David Peck, found his teenagers texting in the middle of the night. He initiated a new rule for his family: at 9:30 p.m. all phones were placed in their charging units in the kitchen and could not be used without permission until 7:00 a.m. He was also concerned that his teenagers might be texting too much at school, so he worked with his cell carrier to limit phone numbers the kids can use for texting and calling during school hours. These are both great ideas.

  Your teen is not going to like limitations on when and where she can use her technology, so don't expect to win a popularity contest with her on this one. Sometimes we just have to be the parent.

- *Don't allow your kids to provide any personal information in public digital spaces.* Here, the old rules still apply. In your teen's social media closed circle of friends, the risk of sharing personal information is extremely small. But on public digital spaces, such as websites, blogs, or forums, don't permit your teen to post any personal information that would make it easy for a stranger to find him or her. Don't allow their locations to be posted, or where they regularly hang out, where they work, and what time they get off work.

● *Make it clear that you intend to be a "friend" on each of your teen's social media profiles and that you will regularly check the profiles.* Your teen might balk at this expectation, as he or she will want their profile to be private, free from a parent's snooping eyes. This is a completely understandable and normal response for a teen who has a legitimate need for increasing amounts of privacy. But don't give in. This will serve a couple of good purposes: ensuring that your teenager will give some thought on what she posts on her profile, and giving you the opportunity to view content that others post on her profile as well. Resist the urge to make your own comments on your teen's profile, and stay away from posting "likes" to her or her friends' posts.

● *Ask your teens to agree to tell you if they receive any inappropriate or threatening messages, images, or videos.* Your child may receive inappropriate or threatening messages from others—whether uninvited or invited. Set the expectation that you need to know if this occurs so that you can deal with these situations. Tell your kids they will not get in trouble, but that you do want to know. The earlier you have this talk with your teen the better. There is another fine line here, between meddling in a conversation and intervening, so use care in walking that fine line.

The difficult thing about setting media expectations and consequences is that your kids won't always agree with you, and you will likely get old standby arguments like, "I don't listen to the words" or "Everybody gets to watch that movie but me." Here is where you can practice using the words I told you about in chapter three: "I feel your pain," "Nevertheless," and "Life isn't fair." Hold your ground, keep on top of their media use, and dialogue as much as possible.

## REFLECTION QUESTIONS

1. How do you see media influencing teenagers today? Specifically, in what ways do you see media influencing your teenager?

2. What do you consider to be the positive aspects of today's media and the technology that delivers it?

3. How important do you feel it is to oversee and monitor your teenager's media consumption?

4. What is one area of media consumption where you are confident you are setting a good example for your teenager? What is one area where you need improvement?

5. What obstacles do you face in setting clear, appropriate expectations and consequences for your teen's media consumption? How can these obstacles be overcome?

# 6

# Teaching Healthy Sexuality

It just sort of happened. I wasn't
planning on losing my virginity. He
was cute and he told me he loved
me. The next day he pretended
like he didn't know me at school.

**JENNY, AGE FIFTEEN**

Since when is being a virgin
a bad thing? I'm proud of my
abstinence, and I will continue
to wait until I marry.

**SHERRI, AGE FIFTEEN**

*T*HE NUMBERS SURROUNDING TEEN SEXUALITY today are
both hopeful and disturbing. Some good news: the teen pregnancy,
birth, and abortion rates in the Unites States have reached their
lowest level in almost four decades,[1] and the number of teens who
report having had sexual intercourse is dramatically lower than
twenty-five years ago.[2] Now the bad news: 47 percent of teens

between the ages of fifteen and nineteen say they have had sex, and the rate increases with the age of the teenager. Only 18 percent of boys and 13 percent of girls had sex by age fifteen, but by age nineteen, two-thirds of both boys and girls have had sex.[3] Regarding oral sex, the rates of teen involvement are fairly close to those we see with sexual intercourse. In recent years, the US Centers for Disease Control and Prevention found that about 50 percent of teens have had oral sex.[4] According to the CDC, sexually transmitted diseases such as chlamydia, gonorrhea, and syphilis have increased dramatically, and of the 20 million new STD infections each year, the majority affect fifteen to twenty-four-year-olds.[5] In the United States, one in four teens has contracted an STD.[6]

Clearly, the teenager in your home is growing up in a highly sexualized culture. Yet, despite what the media may report, many young people today *do* have the desire to live a life of sexual integrity. Not everybody is "doing it." With the incredible amount of unhealthy influences from the world around them, your teen will have to go against the tide of culture and have the courage to stand for sexual integrity. It won't be easy, but more and more studies are revealing that parental influence and role modeling is one of the major factors in helping teenagers make good decisions about their sexuality and relationships.

Experts with both liberal and conservative ideas on sex education tend to agree that "actual sex education does NOT lead to promiscuity. Children who receive sex education at home are actually less likely to engage in risky sexual activity."[7] In other words, the more positive, healthy, value-centered sex education kids receive at home, the less promiscuous they will be. Miriam Kaufman puts it this way:

So turn off the television and get talking. Having open communications with children about sex and other matters is healthy and safer in the long run. This does not necessarily mean it will be easy or without awkward moments. Teens are still very private people. However, speaking about sex early increases the chance that teens will approach parents when difficult or dangerous things come up.[8]

Many parents are willing to do everything possible to make sure their teen stays pure until his or her wedding day. But locking a teenager in your home from now until the day of the wedding isn't realistic. Intimidating your daughter's boyfriend will only go so far (I cannot confirm or deny whether we tried this with our daughters' dates). While the idea of helping to preserve your teen's chastity is noble, we can and should do so much more for our kids. We can help them establish habits of sexual integrity that extend throughout their lifetime.

The Bible speaks clearly about sexual purity, and for good reason. It is ultimately for the health and well-being of our relationships. If your teen commits to a lifestyle of sexual integrity, it will help his or her marriage and family in the long run. How many wives and husbands do you know who still carry baggage in their marriage from unwise decisions about sex and relationships in their younger years? I'm afraid there are too many to count. I've spoken and written about marriage for years, and I'm always amazed at how often sexuality is a key factor in a broken relationship. This is why I encourage young people and their parents to live by what I've called the Purity Code. Here is the commitment I challenge teens and their families to make:

## The Purity Code Pledge

In honor of God, my family, and my future spouse, I commit to sexual purity.

This involves:

- Honoring God with my *body* (1 Corinthians 6:20)
- Renewing my *mind* for the good (Romans 12:1-2)
- Turning my *eyes* from worthless things (Psalm 119:37 NLT)
- Guarding my *heart* above all else (Proverbs 4:23)

Choosing to live by the Purity Code is the opposite of what's promoted in today's sexualized culture, where teens go from one sexual partner to the next. Your teen will need all the help and guidance possible.

Many churches and youth ministry organizations provide events where teens are challenged to commit themselves to a life of purity. I've seen thousands of teens take this pledge and strive to follow through on their commitments. Special programs like these can spark good conversations with your teens, but honestly, nothing is more effective than when parents have conversations with their kids about healthy sexuality. You can do this! Part of your job description as a parent is to take a proactive approach to communicating with your teens about sexual integrity. Don't forget, you are the most influential person in your teen's life. It might be awkward, but your influence is the most important.

## THE TALK

Parents often ask me about the right age to have "the talk" with their teenagers. I always give the same answer: "Never." A one-time birds-and-bees talk doesn't work. Whether it's about sex or any other issue important in our teens' lives, we need to create an open, trusting environment of healthy dialogue, so that when they need answers, they feel comfortable talking with us. When it comes to discussing sexuality and relationships with our kids, preaching and lecturing just doesn't work, especially if sexuality hasn't been discussed in your home before. The "don't have sex until you're married" edict is certainly a clear message, but it will not have as much weight in your teen's decision-making process as a series of ongoing conversations.

You might think your teen will tune out your advice about relationships and sex, but studies show that teenagers view their parents as the biggest influence on their sexual behavior. This means parents are more effective and important than friends, media, educators, siblings, or even the church. Even so, young people today turn to the Internet for information on sex more than any other resource. Do you really want to trust Google as your teen's key provider of sex education?[9]

Talking about sexuality is rarely ever comfortable for a parent or a teenager. It's awkward. Tweens and young teens are especially mortified by the thought of having such a conversation with their parents. Yet delaying the conversation isn't a good idea: one study showed that almost 50 percent of parents only have an initial conversation about sex with their kids after their kids have already had intercourse. With this in mind, have your conversations early and have them often. In fact, the earlier the better. If you have younger children at home, I encourage you to start conversations with them now.

The following is a simple way of looking at what to talk about and when, based on age-appropriate developmental research. In my research for my Pure Foundations book series for kids on healthy sexuality, I learned that parents waited far too long to have these conversations.[10] I've included childhood and preteen information to give you an idea of the natural progression of sex-related discussions.

- *Ages three to five—God made your body.* Teach kids about the parts of their bodies and the fact that one day they will grow up to be mommies and daddies. God created boys and God created girls. Their private areas are different from those of the opposite sex, and their bodies are special.

- *Ages six to nine—How God makes babies.* This is the age of curiosity. Answer their questions in an age-appropriate manner. At this age children are too young to have all the details of the reproductive system spelled out, but it is important for them to hear the basics about their bodies and those of the opposite sex. Because of the prevalence of sexual abuse of children, this is the age to teach them about appropriate and inappropriate touch. If anyone or anything makes them feel uncomfortable, they can talk to Mommy or Daddy. Just because puberty hasn't kicked in at this age doesn't mean their sexuality is not an important part of their development.

- *Ages ten to fourteen—The Purity Code.* This is the best time to present the Purity Code. Help them understand the importance of sexual integrity before they start dating. Talk with your children about how their bodies will change before they actually start to change and then celebrate the changes. Some families have a private family party when their daughters begin having menstrual periods. Rather than being awkward, having a celebration and tradition can normalize this experience. The ages ten to fourteen are very critical to the development of healthy sexual values and building wholesome relationships. Look at this time as a prevention and training in healthy relationships with the opposite sex.

- *Ages fourteen and up—Talk about anything and everything.* By age fourteen, talk with your kids about anything and everything regarding sex and sexuality. The media is shouting a much different set of values than those you want your teens to live by. Many celebrities are not the role models we want our kids following; however, because of the silence of parents on this subject, these people become default role models who influence our teenagers. If you haven't talked about masturbation, oral sex, sexually transmitted diseases, sexting, and other important but difficult issues, know that others will gladly communicate their values with your kids. If you haven't talked with your kids about sex, it's not too late. Just dive in and start the process. There are excellent resources available to help you.[11] But don't wait.

I'm reminded of a cartoon where a father and his son are sitting in a fishing boat in the middle of a lake. The son angrily says to his dad, "You got me out here just so you could have the sex talk with me?" With a sheepish look, the dad says, "Don't get mad, Jeremy. I just thought this might be an opportunity for us to have a frank Q and A session about sex." Jeremy replies, "Okay, fine. I'm sorry for yelling at you. Now, Dad, what do you want to know?" Obviously, that's not how it's supposed to work.

## PORNOGRAPHY CAN TAKE DOWN YOUR TEEN

Pornography is wreaking havoc on the minds and hearts of teenagers today. It's definitely not a feel-good parenting topic, but it must be addressed and discussed with your teen. It's possible you made it through the teen years without viewing pornography. That is probably not the case with your own child. In fact, if your child is a teenager, he's likely already viewed pornography. The Internet and smartphones have revolutionized the delivery of and access to pornography, bringing it right into the lives of every young person in America—even if they only see it by accident. Today, the number one demographic for new users of Internet pornography is boys aged eleven to seventeen. And girls in this demographic are right behind them. Kids first see porn today before the age of twelve, on average.[12] One recent study has found that among thirteen to seventeen-year-olds, 18 percent seek out porn online weekly, and 21 percent come across porn weekly, even when they aren't seeking it.[13]

One problem with porn is that the human brain takes a picture of everything we view, which means that countless teens have pornographic images embedded in their minds. Teens who have viewed porn repeatedly may struggle with the tendency to view the people around them as sex objects. Sex can become nothing more than the sex act, without the physical and emotional intimacy ordained by God since creation itself. Even mainstream secular media is reporting on the long-term negative affects of porn on its users by decreasing men's virility and libido.[14]

Pornography is extremely addictive. Neurological research has revealed that the effect of Internet pornography on the human brain is just as potent, if not more so, than addictive drugs like cocaine or heroin.[15] While no one disputes the dangers of addiction to hard drugs like these, much less is said about the addictive nature of pornography.

Once teenagers view pornography, the practice can quickly escalate in their lives. If you teach your kids to embrace the Purity

Code and the four biblical standards behind the code, it doesn't leave room for porn. Honoring God with your body, renewing your mind for the good, turning your eyes from worthless things, and guarding your heart simply can't be done while regularly viewing pornography. Even so, parents need to be proactive to help their teenagers learn about the dangers of pornography and its stages of addiction:

## STAGES OF PORN ADDICTION

1. *Viewing pornography.* Almost all kids will view pornography, and many will feel ashamed or think it is dirty, even as they find it intriguing and mysterious. The images themselves have a way of drawing us back for more.

2. *Addiction.* Take the brain's power to store images and replay them and add to it the curiosity and sexual awakening occurring in an adolescent, and you can understand how easy it is for young people to become addicted to porn and want to return again and again to images that stimulate them.

3. *Escalation.* As a teen becomes addicted to porn, the brain craves stimulation, just like we see in drugs, alcohol, and gambling addictions, creating a strong desire for the teen to view it more frequently. One young man told me, "I'm hungry for porn. I'd rather watch pornography than eat."

4. *Desensitization.* After addiction and escalation, the mind becomes desensitized to what at first might have bothered the teen. What was gross three months ago or even three weeks ago is now appealing. As with any type of addiction, the mind and the body crave more and look for a stronger high, which in the case of porn can be experiences that are more and more aberrant, vile, and violent.

5. *Acting out.* In the advanced stages of porn addiction, teens act out the images in their mind, engage in fantasy communications with like-minded peers (texting, messaging apps, online forums, etc.), and eventually want to act out what they have seen with another person.

Sexual addiction is a growing problem among young people, and pornography is the main culprit. This is why it is so important to have ongoing conversations with our teenagers about sexual purity and integrity, with the goal that they will be able to talk about what they have seen and seek help.

Accountability is one of the key ways to overcome porn addiction. Whether it is with porn or another sensitive subject, it is usually difficult for a parent to be their child's accountability partner. Encourage your teens to have accountability relationships with both peers and trusted adults. Because teen porn addiction has become so prevalent in our culture, resources have been created to help. There are great organizations available to help provide protection through accountability tools and to walk alongside addicts through the steps of recovery.[16]

## SEXTING: THE NEW FIRST BASE

Ranking right up there with porn is sexting. Sexting is sharing nude or seminude photos or videos, typically using a smartphone. A recent study found that sexting is the new norm among adolescents, and isn't reserved for kids typically involved in at-risk behaviors.[17] As shocking as it may be to parents, sexting is considered the new "first base" for teens. Another study found that more than half of teenagers reported sending or receiving sexually explicit messages but were unaware of the potential legal consequences of sexting.[18]

In some areas, teenage sexters can be prosecuted for distributing child pornography or other crimes. One teenage boy in California sent his girlfriend nude photos of himself so she would do the same thing in return. When he received her nude photo, he thought it would be funny to send it on to a friend. The girl was mortified and the law saw no humor in the situation. The teenager was arrested and subsequently convicted of distributing child porn. He had to register as a sex-offender. It's hard to underestimate the damage viral distribution of a sext can cause a teenager.

As a part of normal progress through adolescence, teenagers don't always comprehend the potential consequences of their actions. This makes sexting particularly insidious. Today, ephemeral smartphone apps (like Snapchat) can give teens a false sense of security that a sext will simply disappear from the recipient's phone in a few seconds. But it's not hard to capture a screenshot of a Snapchat message and save it. We're likely all aware of tragic stories where teens' lives have been devastated by a sext that went viral. Such occurrences cause psychological distress. In some cases, teens have taken their own lives as a result.

Let me be clear. It is very important to have conversations with your teens about sexting. And because you likely pay for their smartphone, let them know you have the right to check it from time to time. This doesn't mean that you would necessarily find evidence of sexting on the phone if you check it, even if your teen was involved in it (there are apps available that allow teens to hide photos). But saying that you reserve the right to check your teen's phone, for many, will provide the needed measure of motivation and accountability to avoid sexting altogether.

## WHAT ABOUT DATING?

It sure was easier dealing with kids when boys were yucky and girls had cooties. As the teen years progress the words *yucky* and *cooties* are replaced with *hotties!* It is a natural and even healthy progression for teens to have a growing interest in the opposite sex. For some, it starts early, even before adolescence. One of my daughters was five when she started talking about liking certain boys. She would tell me who she was going to marry. Another daughter was closer to her girlfriends and didn't have a serious crush until college.

Part of helping teens grow up to become responsible adults is to lead them toward a healthy view of the opposite sex. I tell teenagers that they are called to have a *radical respect* of the opposite sex. Paul's advice to the Romans applies to all relationships, including teens interested in dating: "Outdo one another in showing honor" (Romans 12:10 ESV).

Kids today are dating at very young ages. It is good for kids to have positive experiences relating to the opposite sex, but to allow dating at ages twelve, thirteen, or fourteen gives cause for concern. Think about it this way: the earlier a kid begins forming romantic feelings, and begins to date exclusively, the more years she or he will have before reaching adulthood for temptations and opportunities to move toward engaging in sexual behaviors. Conversely, the longer a teen postpones becoming romantically involved and dating exclusively, the more mature he or she will become (we hope) and the fewer years he or she will spend dealing with sexual temptations and opportunities. Some authorities tell us that if a child dates exclusively at age twelve, there is a 91 percent chance that he or she will have sexual intercourse before they graduate from high school. If a teenager waits until age sixteen to date exclusively, there is only a 20 percent chance that he or she will have sexual intercourse before high school graduation.

There are two types of dates—inclusive and exclusive. Inclusive is where a few boys and girls spend time together in a nonphysical, nonromantic experience. Exclusive dating involves a boy and a girl spending time together alone. With the right supervision, inclusive dating is how teens learn best to relate to the opposite sex in healthy ways. However, exclusive dating at younger ages, even if it is not a sexual relationship, can rev up teens' hormonal engines too soon and lead toward early sexualization. Too often, teens make sexual decisions based on emotional involvement that exceeds their maturity levels. I've seen many good kids get in way over their heads and hearts in exclusive relationships at too early of an age.

Remember that we don't teach our teenagers to live by the Purity Code just to keep them away from sex before marriage. That's too low a goal. Rather, it is to help them become responsible, to make wise decisions, to help them enter marriage with less baggage, and to build upon the strong discipline of fidelity and faithfulness it takes to choose sexual integrity rather than our culture's anything-goes lifestyle. Doing this requires open and honest dialogue about anything and everything pertaining to sexuality and relationships. The result is that teens begin to understand that their sexuality is a gift from God and is intended to honor him.

 **REFLECTION QUESTIONS**

1. As a parent, what concerns you most about raising your teenager in our highly sexualized culture? Why?

2. What kind of influence did your parents have—for better or for worse—on your sexual standards? What,

if anything, do you hope to imitate from your parents'
example as you influence your own teenager? What
might you want to change?

3. What topic of sexuality would make you most uncomfortable to discuss with your teenager? Why? What
can you do to help yourself become more comfortable?

4. Do you know whether or not your teenager has
viewed pornography? If so, do you know if it was
accidental exposure or intentional? What steps have
you taken (or should you take) to protect your teen
from the damage of pornography?

5. What do you feel are appropriate dating standards
for your teenager?

# 7

# Ending the Homework Hassle While Preparing for College

Mom, Dad, don't worry.
EVERYONE failed that test.

**KATIE, AGE THIRTEEN**

The human brain is amazing.
It functions 24/7 from the
time we were born and only
stops when we take tests.

**TEENAGER'S POST FROM TUMBLR**

*ANY TIME PARENTS OF TEENAGERS* or preteens are in a room together, the subject of homework and education seems to be on their lips. My experience is that most of the time parents worry more about their teen's schoolwork than the teen does! I'm not promising to improve your teen's grade point average. Actually, before you are finished with this chapter you may have to see your teen's grade point average lowered for a while. But then again, you will have to ask the question, "Is my primary purpose in parenting to help my child become a responsible adult or to get good grades?" If you answered good grades, I think your goal is too low.

A good friend of mine is a university president. He told me that a mom called him to complain about a poor grade her son was getting in a business class. The president wasn't totally sure why she called him, but he did say he would check into it with the professor. When he asked the professor about this particular student's grade, the professor said the student wasn't motivated and had written a terrible mid-term paper. When the president reported his finding to the mom, she was extremely angry and said, "That was not a bad paper, it was an A paper. I have an MBA from Stanford and I wrote that paper for my son!"

Being educated is a teenager's primary job, and school is their workplace. Rather than seeing education merely as a stepping-stone to future employment and to earning a living (it *is* this, of course), it's more important for your teenager's progress toward adulthood that you view it as *his responsibility* during this season of his life. This responsibility should include striving to learn all he can and doing the best he can do academically. A parent should encourage, challenge, and guide him when he does not live up to his academic potential, while remembering that the responsibility is his, not yours.

Some parents mistakenly wrap their own self-image into how their teen performs academically. They cannot live with knowing their teen is doing poorly in school—it is not an option, because it reflects poorly on them. So they do their child's homework themselves. For other parents, it's a matter of family pride. Who hasn't attended a school science fair where it has been obvious that Mom or Dad made their child's project? For still others, it's a matter of practicality, perhaps hoping that a scholarship will pay their teen's college tuition. I understand and sympathize with the many reasons parents have for bailing their teens out academically, but the bottom line is that none of these helps the teen become a responsible adult. Education ought to be a monkey on your teenager's back, not yours.

High school senior Lindsey and her parents were often locked in conflict over homework. Lindsey was a bright girl, but she just didn't apply herself. Her parents would nag, bribe, restrict, shame, and sometimes even do her homework themselves, all so she could keep her grades up and get a college scholarship. Finally, they took Lindsey's monkey—her lack of discipline—off their backs and put it on hers.

They sat down with her and explained that they were partly at fault for all the tension in the home. They admitted that they should be nagging less. Starting then, they would release the homework decisions to her. She alone would experience the consequences of her academic decisions. It was a good talk, but that didn't mean things changed overnight. Lindsey continued to miss homework assignments, and her grades weren't good enough to get into a four-year university. But two years at a community college did bring some maturity, and she eventually became an excellent student, graduating with honors at UCLA.

## HOW TO HANDLE HOMEWORK

In a HomeWord podcast, John Rosemond spoke about his excellent book *Ending the Homework Hassle*, and introduced his ΛBCs for putting an end to family conflict over the issue.[1] It's one of the most freeing plans I've seen for dealing with homework—yet admittedly, it's a difficult one for parents addicted to control. In a strange twist of fate, it turns out that these ABCs are nothing more than the approach to homework many parents used fifty years ago.

A. *All by myself.* Teens ought to be responsible for doing their own homework. Find a private place for your teen to do homework and help set up an environment conducive to study. Then leave them alone. If they flunk the homework assignment, they chose the consequence. We have to teach them independence.

B. *Back off.* This may be the most difficult step for parents. "Backing off" means refusing to give your kids constant attention at homework time. Nagging really doesn't work in the long run. It can become like a constant dripping and a form of torture. John says that about 80 percent of the time, "I need help" means they are looking for someone to fix a problem or bail them out. It's possible to back off from helping the kids do the homework and take on a more supporting and encouraging role. Even if your teen fails the homework assignment, they will learn an important life lesson from the experience. Don't rob them of this learning experience.

C. *Call it quits.* Many parents set a time when kids must begin their homework and a time for them to quit. Set deadlines to finish the work. John strongly advises, "When it's time to quit, it's time to quit." Give your kids plenty of time to get it done, but don't let it become a fight every night that ends up creating a poor family environment. This will give your kids a chance to learn to manage time more effectively.

## LOOK AHEAD

Even as we look at the issue of education and its role in building responsibility in your teenager, it's important to keep an eye on his education beyond the high school years. Most teenagers of parents reading this book will attend college after high school graduation. Will yours? The answer may not be a simple or straightforward as it has been in recent generations.

Ultimately, your end goal is to help your teen become a responsible adult. Keep that in mind as you consider these issues. Pursuing a college education is often the responsible choice, but college isn't for everyone. Just ask Bill Gates.

If college is definitely in your teenager's future, understand that there are many ways to pursue a college education without being subjected to a lifetime of debt. For your child, it may mean choosing to attend a community college for the first two years, and then attending an in-state school for the last two years. A great education can be achieved without attending the best university or the most expensive one.

The bottom line is that parents, together with their teenagers, should get a head start in discussing all of the dynamics that will go into making decisions about education and career paths in the future. If your child is just entering the adolescent years, you have some time to process these things. You don't have to ask your middle-schooler to decide her college major today. But you should absolutely keep higher education on your radar screen. If you believe your child will one day head off to college, it's never too early to begin thinking about how—and who—will finance her education, and begin taking steps, such as establishing a college investment account, to make it possible when the time arrives.

## CHOOSING A COLLEGE

Some time ago I was sitting next to a woman on a plane. I noticed she was diligently working through some college information brochures. I said, "It looks like you have a child ready to enter the college world." She smiled and replied, "Well, my daughter is only nine, but it's just never too early to start with all the pressure to get into the right schools." I was speechless. Early planning is a good thing for college finances, but neither kids nor parents should have the extra pressure to make sure they get everything just right when their child is in the third grade. Many parents know what it's like to feel as though they didn't start saving soon enough for college expenses. I can relate! If we had to do it over again, we would choose to start that process sooner.

We have the privilege of partnering with Azusa Pacific University in the HomeWord Center for Youth and Family, and I called upon our good friend Dr. Jon Wallace, the president of APU, to brainstorm with us on how to help kids make responsible decisions about college. Here is what we came up with:

- *Pray about it.* The college years are typically when a person makes some of the most important decisions in life—chief among them whether or not (and whom) to marry, and what career path to pursue. These are not decisions to be made lightly, so it's important to bathe the college issue in prayer before deciding where and when to attend.

- *Ask others about their experiences.* Scripture reminds us that there is wisdom in the counsel of many (Proverbs 1:5; 15:22). Do you know anyone who is already attending a school your teen is interested in? Get to know them. Ask them what it's like to attend the school. Hearing about a real life experience will tell you more about a college or university than any handbook or brochure ever will.

● *Visit the campus.* This one might sound obvious, but you'd be amazed at the number of teens and their parents who make decisions about where to attend college based only on a brochure, website, or just because it's Mom's or Dad's alma mater. Since college is where your teenager will be spending some of the most formative time of her life, take a couple of days to visit, preferably when school is in session, and walk the campus. Sit in on a class or two. Talk to some of the professors and staff. Really "try the place on."

● *Research possible colleges.* This is another obvious point too many parents miss. Just because you have good memories from your days at "good old State U" doesn't mean it will be right for your teenager. Get the brochures, look at websites, and both you and your teen do your homework.

● *Start saving now.* There's no time like the present. This is especially true when it comes to saving for college. Whether your child is seventeen years or seventeen months, it's never too late (or too early) to start saving for college. Don't try to save the whole amount at once. Save what you can and start doing it now.

● *Remember that grades count.* High school can be a confusing time for young people. One moment, their main priority is getting straight As; the next, it's simply hanging out with friends and having a good time. Many scholarships are based on a student's GPA. So stress to your child the importance of earning good grades and maintaining a solid grade point average. (But remember, it's his primary responsibility, not yours.)

- *Search for scholarship help.* There are plenty of free scholarship search engines available online. It takes some time to search, but millions and millions of scholarship dollars are available. Ask your teenager to invest a few hours a week searching these sites during their junior and senior years of high school. It's worth the investment of time.

- *Apply early to schools.* In many cases, institutional financial aid from a school is given to students who apply and are admitted early. For this reason, it is in your family's best interest to apply early. Some schools actually make the acceptance process a bit easier if you apply early.

- *Meet deadlines!* Many times, state and federal government aid is contingent on a student getting their FAFSA (Free Application for Federal Student Aid) in by a priority deadline. For more information, visit the FAFSA website at fafsa.ed.gov.

As we talk to our teens about college, it's best to help them (1) understand the big picture of how grades and finances affect options, and then (2) take ownership of the decision. In other words, the reality is that we can help our teens attend certain colleges and come out relatively debt-free. There are more expensive/higher-profile universities that they could choose, but they would need to work each summer, do work-study while attending school, and take out student loans. The more they understand, the more well-informed their choices will be.

My wife and I are on the other side of the college and education issue. All three of our daughters have master's degrees and did well in school. (One of them did cram a four-year education into six years, but that's another story.) As we reflect on their education process, we would have done it differently. We would have taken the advice in this chapter and put more of the responsibility on our kids, instead of struggling daily with the feeling that we cared more about their education then they did. All three of our daughters went to four-year colleges out of high school, and now we see the benefit of some kids going to a two-year school, either for financial reasons or simply because they needed to learn some life lessons in high school, including the consequences of poor grades.

*Don't let your kids' education get in the way of teaching them to be responsible adults.* No one said it would be easy. Today you can get the help you need from books, resources, and guidance counselors. Take advantage of the options, and whenever possible, try to end the homework hassle while you prepare your teens for adulthood.

## REFLECTION QUESTIONS

1.  How easy or difficult is it for you to place the responsibility for your teen's education on him or her? Why?

2.  What educational aspirations do you have for your teenager? Would you say these are based more on your dreams for him or her, or on your realistic evaluation? Why?

3.  To what extent have you wrapped up your own self-image in your teenager's academic performance?

4.  Do you agree or disagree with John Rosemond's ABCs for putting an end to family conflict around homework (All by myself, Back off, and Call it quits). Why?

5. What are your feelings about teenagers going to a Christian college? Public/secular university? An Ivy League school? Do you have a plan to discuss this with your teen? Do you have a plan for the financial decisions it will take to get them through school?

# 8

# Keeping the Communication Lines Open

Nobody will listen to you unless
they sense that you like them.

**DONALD MILLER**

My parents when I was seven: "Go to your room!"
My parents now: "Come out of your room!"

**PAUL, AGE SIXTEEN**

*M*OST TEENAGERS CAN KEEP YOU MAD at them 24/7/365. Not only is it a time when they are causing you new worries and concerns, but their communication with you can rapidly deteriorate to one-syllable answers, closed doors, and a desire to keep you at a distance. Teens can text their friends hundreds of times a day, but you often can't get more than a "Fine" out of them when you ask about their day. If younger children are indeed like dogs and teens are like cats, remember that dogs treat you like family, and cats treat you like staff.

When I speak at parenting conferences, I usually ask parents how many of them are enjoying good communication with their teenagers. About 10 percent raise their hands. So if you are having trouble communicating with your teen, you are in the vast majority. When I ask parents if they communicated well with their parents when they were teens, again about 10 percent raise their hands. This doesn't change the communication challenges you face or the possible hurt you experience, but it's good to know you aren't alone.

## ATTITUDE IS EVERYTHING

I tell parents all the time, "You have to take the lead with your attitude. You can't expect your teens to go someplace with their attitude that you haven't gone yourself." *Emotionally unhealthy parents produce emotionally unhealthy kids.*

The Bible talks about inheriting the sins of previous generations to the third and fourth generation. This relates to family attitudes as well. If you were raised in an environment of shame-based parenting, filled with put-downs, pessimism, and disapproval, you will probably have to work harder than others to not repeat the negative pattern with your teenager. But with focus and work, you can be the transitional generation and improve your family's pattern of communication. Keep in mind that creating a positive atmosphere and environment at home is key to your teen's development, and that will have a direct correlation to healthy communication.

If "attitude is everything," then so is atmosphere. How is the atmosphere in your home? If it needs some work, you are in good company with the majority of parents of teens. Far too often the atmosphere in the home is driven by the teen, when what is needed is for the parent to take the lead by setting a better example. This takes discipline and intentionality. If your children see you constantly nagging and criticizing them, don't expect them to enjoy hanging around with you. Teenagers need models of healthy behavior, not criticism. Maya Angelou famously put it this way: "If you have only one smile in you, give it to the people you love. Don't be surly at home, then go out in the street and start grinning 'Good morning' at total strangers." One teen told me, "My mom is constantly criticizing and nagging me, and then when her phone rings, she is totally nice and sweet to someone she hardly knows." You can't mentor and disciple your teen if she lives under your spirit of disapproval all the time.

## ARE WE HAVING FUN YET?

Milton Berle, the great comedian of another period, said, "Laughter is an instant vacation." Long before that, King Solomon shared these wise words, "A cheerful heart is good medicine, but a broken spirit saps a person's strength" (Proverbs 17:22 NLT). So much poor communication with families has little to do with communication technique and much to do with our busy lifestyles and stress.

One of the most effective ways to ruthlessly eliminate stress in a family is to have fun together. Fun and playfulness heal broken relationships and open up closed spirits. When a family laughs and plays together, it is emotionally nourishing.

How is your family's laughter quotient? As kids become teenagers, families have to become even more intentional about having fun together. Play deprivation in families can easily shut down togetherness and communication, bringing hostility and negativity instead. Play and laughter are a release. As my friend and teen expert Wayne Rice likes to say, "If laughter comes easily for your family, getting through the tough times will be a lot easier also."

## DEALING WITH ANGER

A woman was talking to me about her teenager, who was giving her an especially challenging time. "How do I deal with the anger issue?" she asked. I smiled. "Your anger or your daughter's anger?" She paused a moment, then said, "My daughter's, but come to think about it, I'm angry at her much of the time too."

It's always best not to discipline or say things to your teen while you're angry. Just bite your tongue. You don't have to say everything you think. Most of our personal regrets come from what we have said to others in anger. People deal with anger in many ways. Some people stuff it down. Other people rage and scream. Regardless of how we vent our anger, it's important to deal with it. Remember, your kids will learn most how to deal with their frustrations and anger as they watch how you handle your frustrations and anger. We end up saying hurtful things. Parents can also say occasionally silly things, like the parent I overheard say to their nine-year-old, "Do you want me to give you a spanking?" What could the child say? "Well, as a matter of fact I was just thinking about going outside to play, but now that you mention it, maybe a spanking would be a good idea."

## THE POWER OF AN APOLOGY

When you say or do something offensive in your anger, there is great power in immediately admitting it and telling your teen you are sorry. An apology is not a sign of weakness; it is a sign of strength and healthy authority. It's also great role modeling. Saying you are sorry is one of the best ways to model healthy communication for your teen. Someone once said, "An apology is the superglue of life. It can repair most anything." Your teen will know you are not the perfect parent they thought you were when they were five years old. So be proactive, and apologize when needed.

In a podcast interview for HomeWord, author and speaker Gary Chapman talked about five successful ways to apologize. His thoughts are great advice for parents who are looking to build a pattern of healthy communication with their teenager.

1. *Expressing regret.* This is the emotional component of an apology—the "I'm sorry." This is admitting that you've hurt someone and that you are hurting too because you've caused him or her pain.

2. *Accepting responsibility.* This step is often overlooked in today's families, but it is a necessary one for a successful apology. Regardless of whether the hurt was intentional, accepting responsibility means saying, "I was wrong. It was my fault."

3. *Making restitution.* This language takes the apology to another level by asking, "What can I do to make this wrong right?" It demonstrates a willingness to take action to bring healing to the relationship.

4. *Repentance.* This step acknowledges that you don't want the offense to happen again, and that you will take all the necessary steps within your power to see that it does not reoccur. This requires making and implementing a plan.

5. *Requesting forgiveness.* Asking, "Will you forgive me for what I've done to hurt you?" reflects the spiritual nature of your offense. The person you've hurt may choose not to forgive you. You can't force forgiveness, but asking for it is the right thing to do (see Matthew 5:23-24). Whether the person chooses to forgive or not is his or her responsibility, not yours.

These five strategies also give your teen a model and tools to communicate more effectively with an apology. I can't overemphasize the generational nature of poor or healthy communication.

## HANDLING CONFLICT

When you put the words *teenager* and *communication* together, they often equal conflict. Since most of us were never taught how to handle conflict, we tend to do it wrong. We react poorly, or try to avoid conflict altogether. Henry Ford supposedly said, "Most people spend more time and energy going around problems than in trying to solve them." This sure seems to be true for parents of teens.

But not all conflict is bad. Someone once wisely said, "When we long for a life without difficulties, remind us that oaks grow strong in contrary winds and diamonds are made under pressure." There are positive and negative paths through conflict. The negative route is the path of protection—where we seek to protect ourselves from pain and fear. We are closed and defensive, and that leads to power struggles, pain, distance, deadness in the relationship, and a lack of connection. The positive route through conflict is the path of growth. There is an intention to grow and learn. We do not react defensively. We try to understand ourselves and the other person better. We do not necessarily see criticism as an insult to our self-esteem. The result is better connection and understanding. That is what healthy communication is all about with your teen.

## TIPS FOR BETTER COMMUNICATION WITH YOUR TEENAGER

- *Listen more, talk less.* How good a listener are you with your teen? Even when you are convinced that you are right and they are wrong? Listening is the language of love. The easy route is scolding and lecturing, but the results are not the same as when we listen. Sometimes teens just want to talk when they really aren't looking for a parent's opinion. Wise parents will learn to quit answering all of their teen's questions before she asks them! For older teens, it might help if you ask their permission to share your opinion, saying something like, "Would you mind if I shared my perspective?" This sends your teen the clear message that you respect and care for her. When it comes to conflict, John Rosemond has this to say: "The fewer words a parent uses, the more authoritative the parent sounds. The fewer words a parent uses, the clearer the instruction."[1]

Good listening skills include:

- Giving your undivided attention
- Looking beyond the content of the words and paying attention to tone and body language
- Maintaining an accepting and open attitude
- Using good questions to help clarify your understanding

- *Watch your tone and body language when you speak.* Your words only convey part of the message. Your tone and body language usually communicate more than the words themselves. For example, saying "Good job" when your arms are folded across your chest, while you are rolling your eyes and frowning, actually communicates something other than "Good job." Do your best to make sure the message you send is the message you intend.

- *Avoid the silent treatment.* Silence can wreak havoc on communication with your teen. If you need to process your thoughts before you respond verbally, always communicate the purpose of your silence. For example, you could say, "I need some time to consider how to respond. Let's talk about this after dinner."

- *Take a time out when emotions are running amok.* When emotions are at extremes, it's always a good idea to take a cooling-off period to ensure better communication can happen later.

- *Break the no-talk rule before it breaks your family.* Healthy families talk on a regular basis. Both parents and teenagers will experience times when they don't want to talk. That's a given. But make sure these times are the exception, not the rule. Be intentional to create a culture of conversation in your home.

- *Make family mealtimes conversation times.* There is beginning to be a trend of families trying to eat more meals together. But with your family's hectic schedule, it can be tempting to quickly eat and run, moving on to the next activity. So be proactive to go beyond merely eating. Take advantage of having the family gathered together to engage in conversation.

- *Make bedtime conversation time.* One of the best times to have good communication with teens is bedtime. Yes, bedtime. This might not be the optimal time for you, but remember it's not about you. It's about communicating with your teenager. And teenagers' body clocks are naturally wired to stay up later. When teens are in bed but not asleep, they will likely be more ready to talk about their day or their problems or whatever is on their mind. This relaxed atmosphere is a springboard for good communication. And these more relaxed conversations are foundational for the other times when you need to have more serious conversations.

- *Have parent-teen dates or hangout times.* By the time kids hit mid-adolescence, they are very focused on their friends and peers. But most are willing to do something fun with their parents; they still like to eat or shop. I recommend having at least a monthly date with your teenager. Let her or him pick the activity. These are great opportunities for casual conversation, and sometimes the time will be right for more serious discussion. But in all cases these experiences will help build a foundation of healthy communication between you and your teen.

- *Walk around the block.* My good friend John Townsend regularly took his sons on walks around the block. At first they would complain, but about the second lap around the block "the floodgates of communication would open." Whether it is a walk around the block, a cup of coffee at a local café, or shooting hoops together, the bottom line is the same: do whatever it takes to keep the communication lines open with your kids.

If your teenager is making communication difficult, or if he makes it clear he wants you to stay out of his life, remember that your presence still matters. Part of your role in communication is to demonstrate care and connection in a way that means something to him. Dads who say they communicate their love for their teen by working sixty hours a week yet seldom connect with their child are just wrong. Moms who constantly say, "Look at everything I do for you," but don't show care and connection in a way their teen understands are doing it wrong.

Communicating is largely about perception. If your teen's perception is that you are unavailable to him, your proximity doesn't matter. To him, you are unavailable. This is why your presence matters. Kids who have a strong sense of connection to their parents are less likely to indulge in at-risk behaviors. So when we think of communicating with teens, it really boils down to relationship.

## REFLECTION QUESTIONS

1. How do you rate your home's atmosphere?

2. How have you seen anger affect communication between you and your teenager?

3. Would you say that you are vulnerable with your teen and quick to apologize? Why or why not? When was the last time you apologized to your teenager? How did this affect communication with him or her?

4. What can you do to become a better listener with your teenager?

5. How can you take better advantage of routine life opportunities (dinnertime, time together in the car, etc.) to improve communication with your teenager?

# 9

# Becoming Students of the Changing Culture

My parents don't realize I'm a
pretty good kid compared to a
lot of teenagers these days.

**TEENAGER'S POST FROM TUMBLR**

There is that awkward moment
when you tell your parents something
funny, but it turns into a life lesson.

**CAROLINE, AGE SEVENTEEN**

*N*OT LONG AGO, a father in Denver hired a stripper to perform at his twelve-year-old son's birthday party. Unfortunately, this type of behavior is no longer as shocking as it might once have been. The problem is that lots of kids are being exposed to warped sexual images every day, over and over, online. We cannot afford to sit back and allow the dark side of culture to become a major influence in our teens' lives. When I speak to teenagers I often say,

"I wouldn't want to be your age. You experience much more negative cultural influences than I did growing up."

When I was growing up, I was free to walk to and from school, roaming along the way to my heart's content. I was free to ride my bike all around our neighborhood. All the neighbors knew each other and watched out for each other. Back then, teens were still teens and certainly experimented with behaviors that weren't good or healthy for them. After all, even in those days, sex, drugs, and rock 'n' roll were part of the teen culture. But compared to what teenagers are facing today, it seemed like a much more benign world back then.

I'm a very optimistic person, but the world today's teens are growing up in is a mess. We can blame it on media, globalization, and a host of other issues, but our culture has robbed teenagers of their innocence. We can discuss it, complain, protest, and fight the status quo, but in the end, as parents, we are the ones who must make the adjustments and fight to keep a biblical worldview in front of our teens.

By the time you are reading this book, new cultural issues and trends will have emerged since I wrote these words. Our culture is changing so quickly that even culture watchers have a difficult time keeping up.

Not all cultural changes are bad. Many are just different. Kids still crave relationships and community—but they will find them in different ways and through different mediums than previous generations did. It's not their fault that society is rapidly changing. And they have to find their way in the world as it is, not as we might hope it could or should be.

Every year Beloit College publishes something they call a "Mindset List." This collection of cultural reference points shows how the older generations have fewer and fewer shared experiences with each new college freshman class. For today's college students:

- Google has always been around.

- If you say, "Around the turn of the century," they may well ask you, "Which one?"

- There has always been "TV" designed to be watched exclusively on the web.

- A tablet is no longer something you take in the morning.

- Having a chat has seldom involved talking.

- They have never seen an airplane "ticket."

- Exposed bra straps have always been a fashion statement, not a wardrobe malfunction.

- Few of their peers know how to write in cursive.

- Kurt Cobain, Princess Diana, Mother Teresa, Jerry Garcia, and Mickey Mantle have always been dead.[1]

My wife handed me a cartoon recently that showed a teenager lying on the floor in his bedroom. He is holding his smartphone, Skyping with his friend on the computer and listening to music at the same time. The TV is on in the background, and many other gadgets are around the room. As he Skypes with his friend, he apparently answers a question about how he is doing, saying, "So bored. What about you?" The response from his friend. "Same." We got bored when we were eleven, fourteen, and seventeen, but we were never their age with the enormous onslaught of an ever-changing culture.

## GETTING YOUR ARMS AROUND SHIFTING MINDSETS

One of the best ways to help your kids navigate the issues of adolescence is to become a student of the culture. The goal isn't to become anticulture critics, but to get your arms around who and what is influencing your teenagers. With this information, you can teach your teens how to discern the effect of the culture on their lives.

As a parent who wants to be a student of the culture and to keep your arms around the shifting mindsets, you will want to look at issues such as these:

- Kids and media use
- New studies showing a link between teen drug and alcohol use and increased sexual activity
- The fact that teen social media users are more likely to pick and choose faith beliefs
- The fact that teens who are bullied in-person and online are more likely to become bullies
- The fact that young teen girls' suicide rate has recently tripled
- The fact that teenage girls now try alcohol before boys
- The fact that texting and driving is more dangerous than drinking and driving
- The fact that alcohol dependence is linked to age of first drink
- The fact that students with a chronic lack of sleep have poorer focus and lower grades
- The fact that adolescents drink too much caffeine
- The fact that most teens who misuse prescription stimulants say they use other people's medication
- The fact that moms have the toughest time when kids are in middle school

- The fact that two in three teenage girls are unhappy with their bodies

- The fact that too-high parental aspirations can hurt their child's school performance

These are but a few of the issues taken from recent headlines. The point is clear: we must keep up with the latest cultural trends and how they are affecting our children. We must read what they read, watch what they watch, and listen to what they listen to. I suggest keeping up with teen culture issues. We all need to get our arms around who and what is influencing this generation, and our kids in particular.

## READ

One of the most effective ways to quickly learn about teenage culture is to read what they read. These days, many teens aren't getting their reading material from traditional media sources such as magazines or books. The hard-copy magazines still exist, and if your teen subscribes to any, by all means take some time to read them. If your teen doesn't subscribe, you can also find them at your local library. Today, most teen and celebrity-focused magazines have established an online presence, and this is where many teens do their reading. There are also many teen websites. Some of the information is pretty raw, but it will be worthwhile to look at some of these sites to understand their influence. You'll find exactly what is front and center in the minds of adolescents, and what you read will give you a handle on what teens are talking about at school.

More options that provide safe and trustworthy information about youth culture can be found online. One of my personal favorites is Walt Mueller's Center for Parent/Youth Understanding (cpyu.org). Walt is one of the leading Christian authorities on youth culture and does an excellent job helping parents navigate the culture from a Christian worldview. I also recommend Common Sense Media (commonsensemedia.org), which provides family guides and reviews for a variety of media sources such as movies, video games, websites, books, and apps. And my friend and colleague at HomeWord Jim Liebelt curates our Culture Blog (homeword.com/culture-blog) where he regularly posts on fresh culture news and issues. Jim also contributes articles to our website, providing insights and advice on what parents can do regarding cultural issues that are affecting teenagers.

## WATCH

A major part of being a student of the culture is to watch what your teen is watching. Whenever your son or daughter is watching a movie, either watch it with them or watch it later. You will often get key insights into the culture, and the movie will give you a new perspective on issues they are thinking and talking about. When you attend sporting, music, or other types of events at your teen's school, notice how your teen interacts with his or her friends and pay close attention to how other teens their age act as well—what they talk about and wear and how they typically behave. (Don't overtly snoop on them. Just be intentionally observant.) Be the parent who volunteers at youth activities or chaperones or drives. In the field of youth ministry, we called it "contact work." We can learn so much about our kids when we are on their territory.

## LISTEN

Listening is the best way to understand your teen and his or her cultural influences. When our kids were teens, I learned quite quickly that they didn't want me to act like a teenager and participate in their activities. However, it was okay to ask about what was happening in their world—as long as the questions weren't judgmental. Find times to ask your teen casual questions about school, music, drugs, alcohol use on campus, and any other issue. The more casual you are the better! If you get too serious and judgmental or start to lecture based on their answers, you will lose them quickly. Humor, cheerfulness, and enthusiasm help kids to open up.

## WHAT CAN PARENTS DO?

Taking a walk through the teen culture can cause deep concern, but with the right attitude, it doesn't have to. It does take more energy and time to help this generation of adolescents. Teens are growing up in an amoral (and, at times, immoral) culture. This is somewhat of a new phenomenon. In generations past, the biblical worldview was the accepted standard. Not everyone followed it, but if they deviated from it, they recognized they had done something wrong. Today, parents can't give up and they can't back down. You can make a difference when you are proactive.

*Set parental standards.* When it comes to culture, help your teen set standards and develop a sound biblical grid in which to measure morals and values. You can't make everything a fight, but teens who become healthy, responsible adults often say that they understood their parents' expectations. They received clearly expressed expectations about behavior, and they knew the consequences ahead of time. Parents can promote restraint and teach their kids a biblical worldview, but it will take intentionality.

Teens aren't always going to agree with everything a parent says, but they must know your boundaries and your standards, even if they rebel. Most kids really do want to please their parents, despite not always acting like it.

*Teach your kids to discern.* It is better to teach your teen how to discern culture's impact than to keep her in a protective bubble. When kids are younger, parents must truly protect their children from unhealthy cultural influences, but as they become teenagers, your parenting style has to change from protection to what looks more like a coaching relationship. If you keep your kids in a bubble, that bubble will burst when they are outside the four walls of your home and have more freedom. My kids would say that Cathy and I were quite conservative when it came to media. We had plenty of discussions where they thought we might have stepped out of the 1800s. However, we let them see certain movies and TV shows as long as we went along and could dialogue afterward about the content.

You are the parent, which makes you the leader. Good leaders are good listeners, and listening is the language of love. Listening to your kids' opinions honors them, even if at the end you agree to disagree. You may have to say words like, "When I was your age I would have felt the same way, but nevertheless in our home we will do it this way." Teaching our kids discernment keeps the end goal in mind.

*Use experiential learning to help change their lives.* The teenage years are an experimental period. To one extent or another, teenagers are going to distance themselves from the authority figures in their lives, and they'll likely begin thinking they are invincible. "It won't happen to me" is often their motto as they experiment with extreme behaviors.

My advice is to leverage this experimental phase by directing it toward positive experiences. I remember a father sitting with me and telling me how self-centered his son had become. His son was lazy and had a bad attitude, and the dad was at his wit's end. I suggested he take his son on a mission and service project to Mexico sponsored by our church. People were needed to go with some students to help build an orphanage. They would have to sleep on a hard cement floor. The food would be lousy and they wouldn't be able to take a warm shower all week. The son was hardly enthusiastic about the trip, but his dad signed them up anyway.

The dad called me up after the experience and talked about seeing what he called a miraculous transformation in his son. The trip seemed to throw off the boy's life equilibrium. He worked hard, played with the children in the village, was engaged in church services, and bonded with his dad in a way that had not happened in a long time. The dad gave his son an experience that stretched and challenged him. It was a breakthrough experience. Not all stories end up this way, but for this young man it was the catalyst for a change of heart. Experiential learning works with kids and all of us. Today, that young man works for a relief organization helping the poorest of the poor.

*Encourage positive peer influence.* Peer pressure doesn't always have to be negative. Positive peer influence is a very powerful influence. The Bible says, "Bad company corrupts good character" (1 Corinthians 15:33), but the opposite is also true: good company encourages good character.

Healthy friendships will help your teen deal with unhealthy cultural influences. Do everything you can to know your teen's friends and to help foster positive activities at school, church, and elsewhere. Studies show that young people who are engaged with positive activities and a positive school environment tend to have much more strength to overcome negative cultural temptations. This is why I love church youth groups. They can provide a fun, spiritually strong environment with healthy role models and the opportunity for quality friendships.

I had a best boyhood friend, Terry Terrell. We had been Little League buddies and played sports together in high school. During our senior year over Christmas vacation, I brought Terry to a Christian retreat where he made the most important decision of his life—to become a Christ-follower. That one youth ministry experience determined much about his life and his relationship with God. Some years ago, Terry lost his battle with cancer. But his friendships, vocation, marriage, children, and so much of his life were centered around the courageous decision he made one New Year's Eve, with his best friends by his side. Never underestimate the power of positive peer influence.

***Foster spiritual growth.*** Adolescence is a season when teens often question their faith and drift from church. Teens who develop their own spiritual disciplines and stay involved in church are much less vulnerable to at-risk behaviors. Remember, you can't live out a spiritual life for your teen. Nagging them into a deeper relationship with God has never worked, *ever*. However, building a home environment that fosters spiritual growth and gives your kids plenty of opportunity to mature will give them the opportunity to apply their own faith to the culture. Don't give up on them. Teens can be extremely committed to developing and maturing their spiritual life despite the cultural pressures they face—but keep in mind that their faith may look different than yours.

## REFLECTION QUESTIONS

1. What are the biggest changes to youth culture since you were a teenager?

2. What are the biggest obstacles to becoming a student of the culture?

3. From a practical standpoint, what does the challenge to read what they read, watch what they watch, and listen to what they listen to look like?

4. What clear expectations and consequences do you currently have in place regarding your teen's interaction with culture? Do you feel you need to make any changes or additions to these? Why or why not?

5. How can you help your teen channel his or her desire for experimentation toward more positive experiences?

# 10

# Finding Intimacy in Your Marriage as You Raise Your Teen

I ran too fast, too far, too long on too many borrowed miles. And then it hit me like something just plain awful. I have been a psychological, spiritual, and emotional mess. I need to refine my life, my marriage, and my parenting so I can live again.

**A MOTHER OF THREE TEENAGERS**

I want the kind of marriage that makes my kids want to get married.

**EMILY WIERENGA**

**I**'M JUST NOT CONNECTING WITH YOU RIGHT NOW," are common words from people who are married and raising teenagers. The couples are just trying their best to survive and wishing for a kinder, gentler season in life. They love each other, but if they are really honest, they aren't sure if they are "in love." Or, at least, it doesn't feel like it used to. They are tired most of the time. Their conversations seem to center around the kids, and now that the kids are teens, they have more worries. One mom confided, "I just have a genuine sadness deep inside me. I didn't think it would turn out this way. My husband is a good man, but he isn't my soulmate. I would never leave him, but I guess I've just settled for a lifestyle with little connection, and deep inside of me I have sorrow."

You may or may not be feeling like the couple I just described. You may be wondering why I would have a chapter on marriage in a book about raising teenagers. This isn't a marriage book, and many single parents do a great job raising teenagers. But I have found that for many couples, navigating the teen years plays havoc on their marital relationship. Some who have already raised teens tell me it was the most difficult time in their marriage. Yet the quality and example of your marriage will have a profound influence on the life of your teenager. Couples who can navigate the turbulent waters of marriage during the teen parenting years will provide their kids with a foundation of security and peace that will help them enter adulthood as responsible adults who look forward to a healthy marriage themselves.

Jenny and Brad are missing that connection in their marriage. On the outside, they are an amazing couple. They have three beautiful teenagers, and from the looks of their Christmas card and letter, they are the perfect family. Todd is nineteen, Andrew is sixteen, and Ashley is thirteen. Todd was a star athlete in high school and graduated with honors. Andrew is following in his brother's footsteps and his father's before that. Ashley is the princess of the family and has her mother's good looks and her father's charm. Jenny helps lead the school's PTA, teaches a Bible study at her church, and hasn't missed any of her kids' games or gymnastic tournaments. She has a part-time home-decorating business, and people marvel at how she juggles it all. Brad runs a successful business and managed to coach the boys in all their sports. At times, he misses a few gymnastic events, but even then he makes sure to call or text Ashley before and after the meets. These are impressive people with the best intentions. But behind the Christmas letter and perfect family photo, trouble is brewing.

Jenny and Brad are living parallel lives. They are exhausted most of the time. No one is managing the bills very well, and even though they make a lot of money, their debt has piled up. They can't remember the last time just the two of them went away for a replenishing time of romance. Life centers on the kids, work, and everyday commitments and responsibilities. They crawl into bed each night, six inches away from each other but miles apart. The word that best describes how they feel toward each other is *numb*. As for the kids, each has at least one major issue. Todd is a nice young man, but two months into college, he got a DUI that will be on his record for the next ten years. Andrew has been caught smoking pot and visits porn sites regularly. Beautiful Ashley has the beginnings of an eating disorder. The Christmas photo and letter was only half this family's story.

Jenny and Brad have another five to seven years parenting an adolescent. They might be looking ahead, counting on reconnecting after the storms of adolescence move out. But while their marriage is suffering, they are also missing out on opportunities to model a healthy relationship to their kids—not to mention creating the kind of intimate marriage that was always their dream.

Most marriages don't end because of abuse, adultery, or addictions. More commonly, they just fade away. The couple quits paying attention to the basics of a healthy marriage, and drift from each other because of the many distractions around them. One day they look up and see a marriage that is lost.

Again, this book isn't about marriage. Even so, most single parents would agree that it would be easier to handle the teen years with a spouse. This season with teens seems to bring extra tension and stress into a marriage. Instead of a couple leaning into each other, they tend to grow apart. It does not have to be this way.

Let's look at the stressors of a marriage during the teen years and how to overcome them.

## SMOLDERING STRESS

Has stress and busyness pushed your life and marriage into the danger zone? Many families with teenagers are living life at 120 percent. Physician and author Richard Swenson described this situation in a HomeWord podcast. "Today, most of us routinely spend 20 percent more than we have, whether in money, time, or energy," he said. "When life is continually maximized, however, there is no margin for priorities, relationship, depth, worship, rest, contemplation, service, or healing."

Everything is more dangerous at high speed, and eventually, if we continue life at a fast pace, something is going to spin out of control and crash. Often it is the marriage, the kids, and our relationship with God. Normally these should be our three top priorities, but crisis-mode living and stress tend to smother what's most important. It would be better for families to live at 80 percent and have margin for the unexpected. Living with margin takes some of the most focused discipline you can imagine, but it is possible to make the necessary changes.

Jillian's husband wasn't taking the lead in this regard, so she did. Without lecturing or nagging, Jillian made three decisions that brought back a sense of rhythm to the family and her marriage. She established a nonnegotiable date night with her husband every week. She would have loved for him to come up with the idea, but he just wasn't the type of guy to be proactive in this area of their relationship. Then she let the kids choose only one extracurricular activity each season, instead of all the activities and "stuff" that had the family running around so much. Finally, she made Sunday a very different-looking day of the week for the family—a much more restful day.

Jillian's husband wasn't opposed to the date night idea at all. She made sure the kids were set on those nights and planned fun and enjoyable dates that quickly become the highlight of the week and rekindled their romance. The kids first pushed back at participating in fewer activities, but Jillian stood her ground. There were more family dinners and less stress almost immediately. The most difficult change for the family was making Sunday a day of rest. When Jillian was growing up, her family held to a strict Sabbath, which means *rest*. Even as a child she looked forward to a family meal after church on Sunday, and then a slower pace for the rest of the day. So for her own family, Jillian instituted a "technology fast" as part of their Sunday routine. Smartphones would stay in their chargers except for emergencies, and tablets and laptops were off-limits except for schoolwork. As much as possible, they made Sundays family fun days. There were still ups and downs for the family each week—stress didn't disappear—but Jillian's initiatives helped to nourish their relationships, and the family slowly reestablished margin.

Busyness can seem unavoidable in today's world, but it can easily become a habit that takes over a family's life. You look up one day and realize that you have quietly and unintentionally been disconnecting from those you love the most, including God, and replaced what is precious with whatever is most pressing. When we are tired and exhausted, discouragement creeps in more easily. Are you taking care of your own soul? What are you doing to care for your marriage? Do you have replenishing relationships around you to support you and keep you accountable when needed?

There was a time in the prophet Elijah's life when he was so tired and discouraged that he wanted to just give up (1 Kings 19). What did he do? He went to sleep. After he slept, God sent an angel to give him something to eat and drink, and then he went back to sleep again. Only after he was rested and refreshed was he ready to take on the day. Maybe, like Elijah, we need to get more rest.

## REKINDLING ROMANCE

Couples with teenagers around the house often roll their eyes when the subject of romance is brought up. They look back at another time in the relationship as a time with more physical intimacy. Too many couples have settled for mediocrity in their marriage, and frankly, are often just lazy when it comes to romancing each other.

It seems like back in the days when we were dating and courting our spouse, we could always find time and energy for them. We did special little things for them. Romantic love does change over the years, but it doesn't have to slow to a crawl. However, someone in the relationship is going to have to decide to *initiate romance*. Yes, this sounds a bit unromantic and not spontaneous. If the romance in your marriage is good now, then by all means keep doing whatever you are doing. But if it is not working how you want, be more intentional.

When the kids were younger, you could put them to bed early, perhaps light a fire in the fireplace, then get up and go get little Janie a drink of water, go back to the fireplace and snuggle up to your spouse . . . who had already fallen asleep. Yes, you were both tired then too! With teens, you may well be going to bed earlier than they do now. I know a couple who took massage classes together at the local community college. They put a lock on the bedroom door. There have been moments when their teenagers have teased them but frankly, they are being good role models for their kids and their future spouses. A regular nonnegotiable date night is a must. Cathy and I chose to go away for one night each quarter. It's amazing what just a few hours away can do to replenish your relationship. Concerts, walks in the park, flowers, special meals, love notes, texts, and phone calls are all a part of being proactive about romance. The good thing about teenagers is that they can usually take care of themselves, so it is easier to find special times with your spouse.

## MONEY: THE BIG STRESSOR

My father used to always say, "The best things in life aren't things." In the midst of saving for college and weddings, as well as just trying to keep the family budget working, money is one of the major stressors in a marriage with teens at home. The majority of people choose debt over financial freedom. What they may not be thinking about is that debt will cause pressure on a marriage like few other stressors. One couple with teens told me, "We are drowning in debt." As they explained further, it became evident that their marriage was going under because of heavy debt in addition to all the pressures of raising teens.

Do whatever you can and make every sacrifice possible to pay down your debt. No one ever slips out of debt—they crawl. It takes time and discipline, but it's well worth it on several levels, including your marriage.

When Barry and Sharon bought a great house with a larger monthly payment than they could really afford, they didn't realize the extra strain it would place on their marriage. They were already juggling needy kids and a needy mother-in-law, yet what kept them awake at night was the house payment and all the related upkeep. When they finally went to a marriage counselor, he promptly suggested they see a financial consultant from their church. When the consultant asked about their budget, they said they didn't have one in writing but "pretty much" knew how they spent their money. After putting together their budget, there was still no margin. Barry and Sharon basically had two choices. Both of them already worked full time, so either Barry could get a second job or they could move to a cheaper home. Before they made a decision, the financial counselor said, "Don't just look at making your payments. Look at the quality of life with your kids and your marriage." In the end, they sold their home, moved into a smaller rental, set up a budget that allowed 10 percent for giving and 10 percent for saving, and paid off most of their bills. They now say it was the best decision of their marriage. "I grieved about giving up my dream of that house, but our kids really don't care, and Barry and I have our marriage back on track," Sharon said. "We didn't realize how much negative energy we were putting into our financial struggles."

When faced with spending more than you make versus investing in your marriage and family, choose what's most important. Be a faithful steward of your resources. Do what it takes to steer clear of financial burdens. If it means moving to a smaller house or driving a cheaper car or taking a camping vacation rather than an exotic one, by all means do what you can to stay free from bondage or debt. Delayed gratification is the key to financial maturity.

## THE SANDWICH YEARS

Bob and Megan are in the midst of what some would call the terrible teen years. Their son is struggling with ADHD and is medicating his problems with drugs and alcohol. Their daughter is constantly at odds with Megan. It's a tension-filled home. On top of it all, Megan's mother has Alzheimer's and has moved in with them. Like many married couples with teens, Bob and Megan are sandwiched between two needy groups: their teens and their aging parents.

Whenever I do premarital counseling, I always spend some time focusing on the couple's extended family. At some point, I typically ask, "Have you ever thought about what you'd do if one of your parents needed to move in with you and you'd have to take care of them?" The looks and responses are often priceless, and sometimes very amusing. I rarely hear anyone say yes. But I know that by the time they are married and their children hit the teenage years, there's a good chance there will be some in-law issues to negotiate as a couple.

Still, as people trend toward living longer, more and more parents are raising their teens while also helping their own aged parents. With this in-law issue in mind, it's important to talk about and establish expectations with your spouse. Of course, you can't come up with all the answers ahead of time, but the more you talk through things and get on the same page, the better.

Cathy and I had this experience. During this season, it was important for us to talk with each other, set boundaries, and share our mutual needs and expectations. And we needed to do the same with our kids. Teenagers tend to think about themselves more than you or their grandparents or other family members. What they need to see is a united front whenever possible, even as they see you model love and commitment to your extended family.

## LACK OF SPIRITUAL INTIMACY

It's a common surprise: parents think that once their children get past the exhausting toddler years and become more independent, life will slow down and the couple will have more time to connect spiritually. For many, the opposite happens. For whatever reason—busyness, tension in the relationship, stress, or some other issue—couples can grow apart and miss out on spiritual intimacy.

Cathy and I met on our first day of school at Azusa Pacific University. We were married one week after Cathy graduated. From the beginning, we knew we wanted to focus on doing youth and family ministry together. A year later we moved across the country so I could go to graduate school. With hearts united in ministry, we expected to have spiritual intimacy in our relationship. It didn't happen. We had good intentions—we tried everything from devotionals to prayer commitment times and couples' Bible studies. We would usually start out strong—but then we would fail to have the discipline to continue. As our kids got older, our spiritual time together became scarce. We experienced what many couples experience in marriage: the spiritual intimacy in our relationship was our least developed area of intimacy. In many ways, we were leading parallel lives spiritually, yet we knew we were missing something as a couple.

One day we were talking with an older couple who had mentored us from time to time, and we shared our frustrations with them. We expected they were the type of people who read through the Bible every year together and had long intimate prayer times daily. "Actually, you both might be setting yourselves up for failure," they said. "We spend twenty to thirty minutes a week in a devotional time together as a couple. Start with that and see how it goes." The conversation had a huge effect on us. Today, in addition to trying to pray together daily, we set aside a special time each week to focus on spiritual intimacy. We look at a Scripture together, read something short and inspirational, share our ideas about what we've read, and then pray. Our weekly times of spiritual connection even led us to write a devotional for couples called *Closer*.[1] It is the bestselling book at HomeWord, but what is a bit humbling when we hear wonderful testimonies of couples' new found spiritual connection is that they mostly mention the time together, not the book! So why not take the "*Closer* challenge" and commit to spending twenty minutes a week in devotions together?

Dr. David Stoop, a leading authority on marriage, estimates that just one-tenth of one percent of couples who pray together will get a divorce.[2] We're not trying to turn this into legalism, but having a devotional time once a week and praying together daily builds a foundation of spiritual intimacy that will draw couples closer and prepare them for life together—even with teens. Because Cathy and I often come at parenting from different angles, devotional times help to keep us on the same page. So, make it a goal to move toward spiritual oneness. Jesus quoted the Old Testament when he said, "A man will leave his father and mother and be united to his wife, and the two will become one flesh" (Matthew 19:5; Genesis 2:24). If this is your heart's desire—to become one—do what it takes to connect physically, emotionally, *and* spiritually.

For many couples, the goal is to simply *get through* the teen years. But it doesn't have to be this way. The success of your marriage is not the result of marrying the perfect person or always experiencing "the spark." Your success will come from working on your relationship, persevering, and striving to do what is right. A successful marriage does not materialize out of thin air. It takes a lot of hard work, and feels more like an achievement. For sure, it is a blessing from God! And your teenagers will certainly reap the direct benefits of experiencing the security provided by your marriage, and the example of a healthy, God-honoring relationship you are setting for them.

## REFLECTION QUESTIONS

1. What kind of example are you setting for your teenager in your marriage? What areas have room for improvement?

2. What aspects of raising your teen cause conflicts in your marriage?

3. What is biggest cause of stress in your marriage right now? What can you do to reduce this stress?

4. What are you doing right now to make your spouse feel special and to keep the spark in your marriage alive?

5. How are you doing with spiritual intimacy in your relationship? Are you willing to take the "*Closer* challenge" and spend twenty minutes a week being intentional about it?

# 11

# Dealing with a Troubled Teen

I am who I am. I like what I like.
I love what I love. I do what I want.
Get off my back and deal with it.
It's my life, not yours.

**TEENAGER'S POST FROM TUMBLR**

I hate you. I hate Jesus.
Leave me alone.

**TRACY, AGE SIXTEEN**

*O*NE OF THE MOST DIFFICULT THINGS in life is to watch your child making poor choices. It can drag the whole family into emotional, spiritual, and even physical chaos. Every day I hear from desperate families who are looking for ways to help their troubled teens. The parents are literally sick with worry, frustration, and anger. Keep in mind that it's actually normal for teens to become secretive and argumentative and experimental in their behaviors.

The challenge is figuring out what is normal adolescent behavior, what behaviors cross the line into willful rebellion, and what behaviors signal deeper issues where help is needed.

Some kids skate through adolescence seemingly untouched by the problems of the world, while others take the rocky road, with steep hills to climb and dangerous curves at every turn. I see very good parents who have troubled teens and really struggling parents whose kids are amazingly healthy and stable. It would be great if we could clearly point to a certain parenting style or strategy that is fail-proof. Sure, there are trends that show that kids tend to struggle more often under certain parenting styles, but like I said, good parents still have kids who make poor decisions.

If your family has been in crisis or you are dealing with a troubled teen, you know the depth of pain and the burden you carry. Some of the worst heartaches and anguish in our lives come from our kids' poor choices. At times, we've blamed ourselves, our spouses, a divorce, the culture, and even our churches. I've sat with hundreds of brokenhearted parents, so worn down by their teens that they don't know how they can make it through the week. I get it! When a teen makes poor choices, it rips your heart out of your body.

Few parents see it coming. A teen typically evolves with a bad decision here and a poor choice there. Then a misstep takes him in a horrible direction, and a troubled teen emerges. The next thing you know, your reality is different than you ever imagined possible.

Cathy and I have a friend who is a noted author and speaker in the area of youth and family. We know him well. He and his wife are people of integrity, role models for Christian leadership inside and outside their home. Yet their children have struggled with drug abuse, sexual promiscuity, eating disorders, and even arrests. My friend once admitted to me that he was stunned by the way things have turned out with his kids. It has affected his marriage, his vocation, and his health. Sure, a few bumps along the road were to be expected. We've all experienced those. But he and his wife were in youth and family ministry, and they fully believed their kids would turn out similar to the strongest leaders in his youth group. Not so. Whenever I see this couple, we sit and catch up. They have really suffered, and there is a general sadness in their countenance. Frankly, they tried everything I will suggest to you in this chapter. Their kids have been on antidepressants and gone through drug rehab, in-depth counseling, and intense Christian recovery programs. But the struggle remains.

Still, life is not unbearable for them. Even though life hasn't turned out the way they thought or hoped it would, they continue to hold out hope, believing that the story is not finished yet.

There aren't simple answers for dealing with a troubled teen. However, through the years I have seen enough good stories and victories to not be discouraged.

If you have a troubled teen, I want to shout this from the rooftop: there is hope! I see parents every day who work a plan and whose teens turn around their lives and use the bump (or bumps) in their adolescent journey to become stronger and more successful lives than their parents ever dreamed.

Take Jack, for example. Jack was never an easy child. At his first-grade parent-teacher conference, his teacher reported that Jack was extremely smart but had difficulty focusing on his work and didn't always get along with his classmates. Even so, he was very likable, she said, and would probably do just fine. Except that he didn't. The hyperactivity and lack of focus caused more and more problems, and a pediatrician finally diagnosed Jack with ADHD. His parents tried to keep him off medication, but eventually he was put on

Ritalin. As Jack got older, things continued to go downhill. Fights with other boys and lack of respect toward his parents became a way of life. One day, Jack and his father squared off, and Jack took a swing at his dad, yelling, "I hate this f***ing family, and I especially hate you!" The out-of-control behavior resulted in Jack being sent to a boarding school in another state. There he started using marijuana, which led to other types of drug use. At the end of the school year, Jack moved back home and barely made it through the rest of high school. He tried community college, but dropped out the first semester and moved in with a girlfriend. His parents said that as much as they were upset about Jack's poor choices, with him out of the house, their home finally felt physically and emotionally safe. Over the years, they had tried counseling, boarding school, tough love, easing his restrictions, prayer groups—anything that might help.

One day, Jack's girlfriend told him she had been going to a Bible study at work and had renewed her commitment to God. With God's help, she was going to try to stop abusing drugs and alcohol. And she wanted Jack to deal with his addictions to drugs, alcohol, and pornography. Then she told him she was going to live with her aunt, who would encourage her renewed faith. Jack was stunned. He felt rejected, and over the next few weeks he went on a drinking spree. His life got so bad that, just like the prodigal son in the Bible, Jack showed up at his parents' home one day. They lovingly allowed him to stay, but only under the condition that he get help. They set up healthy boundaries and a very short list of expectations, with grace and consequences.

Today, Jack is happily married and has two children. He is a pastor and works with rebellious kids and hurting families. He is very open about his life and shares that he is still dealing with baggage from those rebellious years, and that he must work a plan for the rest of his life for sobriety as well as emotional and spiritual health. As you might expect, though, his parents see Jack's amazing recovery as nothing short of answered prayer. Jack and his wife live near his parents, and enjoy a close relationship with them. Jack says, "If I can find healing, anyone can."

There are countless stories of out-of-control teens who are now living healthy, productive lives. They didn't immediately respond to help when they were younger. Perhaps they hated their parents, but they probably hated themselves too. They knew their behaviors were out of control, but they weren't ready to change. The answer usually lies in the fact that a courageous parent or parents did the right work to help the child get to a place of healing.

## WHAT CAN PARENTS DO?

Many parents experience recurring conflict with a troubled teen. If your home feels like an emotional war zone, know that you are not alone and you are not imagining things. Ongoing tension affects every aspect of the family and strains every relationship.

When your child is going through a difficult season, refer to the same strategy I mentioned in the preface of this book: *Stay calm, be proactive and intentional, and get as emotionally, spiritually, and physically healthy as you possibly can.*

***Persevere and seek God's help.*** Jesus spoke more about trouble and suffering than he did about happiness. The challenges of a prodigal child can tax parents to the very end of their strength. The answer lies in living one day at a time and persevering through life's darkest hours with the power of God's compassion and mercy. The Bible is clear that even in life's most painful and difficult times, we can keep going because God is with us. His mercy endures forever.

I especially love Psalm 136, which reminds me that through tough times we can "give thanks to the Lord, for he is good. *His love endures forever*" (verse 1, emphasis added). Ruth Graham, an amazing woman of God and wife to evangelist Billy Graham, once wrote a prayer in the midst of tough times with her own children. She called it "A Mother Is Praying."[1]

> Listen, Lord
> a mother's praying
> low and quiet:
> listen, please.
> Listen what her tears
> are saying,
> see her heart
> upon its knees;
> lift the load
> from her bowed shoulders
> till she sees
> and understands,
> You, who hold
> the worlds together,
> hold her problems
> in Your hands.

God would never want you to go through the burden of a troubled teen alone. Throughout the Bible, he promises to be there for his children. He doesn't promise to take away all our trials and tribulations, but he does promise to walk with us through the darkest of valleys. Many people find comfort in reading through the inspiring songbook of the Hebrew people, Psalms, or the promises of the book of Proverbs. Others find hope and comfort in listening to worship music and filling their hearts with praise. Living with the pain produced by a troubled teen is not the time to turn away from God in disappointment, but as Ruth Graham's prayer says, it is time to put your trust in him and place your teen into his care. He cares deeply about your prodigal teen.

*Find support.* When a troubled teen disrupts the home, too many parents try to hide it. Some look at their child's behavior as shameful to the whole family. The way I figure it, every family struggles and suffers with a family issue at one time or another. *Every family.* We were not meant to carry family burdens alone. Our pride often gets in the way and we don't want to share our pain even with a trusted friend. That just intensifies the pain.

I love the story of the Israelites battling the Amalekites in the Old Testament (Exodus 17). Moses stands on a hill during the battle and raises his hands toward heaven. As long as he holds up his hands, the Israelites win the battle. But when Moses gets weary and lowers his hands, immediately the Amalekites begin to defeat the people of Israel. So Moses makes a really good decision. In his weariness, he allows the people around him to hold up his hands, and the Israelites eventually win the battle. The same illustration applies to parenting a troubled teen. You don't necessarily need to find people who can take your burden away. Usually they can't do that anyway. But they can help you carry your burden. Maybe that means a regular coffee appointment with a mentor from your church, or a parents gathering. All around the country there are support groups for parents of troubled teens. It may not be easy, but my best advice is to seek support. Don't be afraid to talk about your burden.

*Get on the same page with your spouse.* When there is a rebellious teen in the house, it's natural to play the blame game. And the easiest target is your spouse. This is true if you are a single parent focusing on the faults of your ex or if you are married. However, this is not the time to make your spouse's shortcomings the focal point. It is so easy to do, but it will only distract from the more important issues. If a couple has a game plan they can agree on, they will do much better. Many parents have never read a parenting book or attended a parenting class or seminar together. More women read books about parenting than men. I urge couples facing a parenting crisis to get on the same page as they develop a parenting philosophy. This is especially the time when couples need to work off the same blueprint—the saying "United we stand, divided we fall" applies to parenting too. Two united heads, hearts, and mouths are better than one. If you and your spouse can't get on the same page, then make sure you have a philosophy of parenting that you are following.[2]

***Develop a contract for behavior.*** I have seen many parents, worn down from their teenager's out-of-control behavior, seek quick fixes. They want so badly to stop a teen's problematic behavior and regain a sense of peace in their home that they immediately look into sending their teen to a boarding school or rehab facility. Seldom is this the answer. Helping a troubled teen is a process that usually doesn't start with sending them away. I strongly believe that the first step is for parents to develop a contract together with their teen. Sometimes a change in behavior comes through something as simple as putting a road map in front of your child that clearly defines expectations, consequences, and goals. The contract becomes a wake-up call and can stop certain behaviors before they get more out of control and more destructive. Try to create the contract with your child, and express expectations while identifying good and bad consequences for behavior. Put the contract in writing and see what happens. (If you need help developing a contract, I recommend letting a counselor help you.) Kids will more likely support a contract they helped to create. Creating a contract together gives you the opportunity to show more empathy. Make sure you follow through on the contract, or it will be of no value. Gradually (but not too gradually) make the consequences tougher and tougher.

*Get an assessment.* If your child continues to break the contract, get an assessment. An assessment is simply a thorough checkup on whatever situation or problems are going on with your teen and family. It isn't much different than going to your medical doctor to get a comprehensive examination for a health problem. An assessment isn't a long-term counseling commitment. It's trying to get to the root of the issue in order to develop a plan. For example, I used to conduct drug and alcohol assessments of young people in which I would ask several key questions and usually have an answer for the young person and parents in one session. Depending on what the issue is with your teen, an assessment could be as simple as visiting your school counselor for an academic evaluation. A tougher issue might require a much more complex set of evaluations, which may include psychological, medical, and spiritual assessments.

It's pretty amazing to see kids literally transformed because of an assessment that correctly diagnoses a problem. A light turns on in their brain when they and their parents find out about a learning disability or a physical issue that can be addressed. Even with a more complicated diagnosis, just knowing what the issue is and having a plan in place can do wonders for a troubled teen and his or her family.

Not all assessments bring good news. After a very honest conversation with a sixteen-year-old about his smoking pot and drinking, I asked if he wanted to change his behavior. "Not really," he responded. I told him I appreciated his honesty, and I invited him to call me on my cell phone whenever he was ready to change or had hit the bottom. Later, when I met with his dad, I said, "I'm so sorry, but your son is just not ready today to get the help he needs or to make the right decisions about his drug and alcohol use and abuse." We then talked about how to apply tough love to the situation and help create a crisis to motivate the son to reach out for help. Many times, a trained drug and alcohol counselor can help you create the plan for an intervention.

***Seek counsel from an expert.*** Many times, counseling is a good option after an assessment. The Bible says, "Where there is no counsel, the people fall; but in the multitude of counselors there is safety" (Proverbs 11:14 NKJV). Most people who work with troubled teens are really good at what they do and they can give you the counsel you need to bring clarity to the situation.

Some kids who are struggling need a neutral, safe person to talk with, someone who understands what they are going through and can help them get to a better place. Find a counselor who is good with students and has a solid track record working with adolescents; some counselors work better with adults. Make sure your teen can identify with his or her counselor. For most kids going through difficult issues, a professional counselor is best. But don't overlook pastors, youth workers, teachers, and coaches who can positively influence your son or daughter.

Often in these situations, counseling becomes a family affair, and there are certainly times when the entire family should be involved. Keep in mind that parents can benefit greatly from seeking counseling for themselves. Cathy and I have never hesitated to seek the wisdom and counsel of experts. Seeking counseling is a sign of strength, not weakness.

## How to Find the Right Counselor for Your Situation

- *Ask a trusted friend or pastor for a recommendation.* People who have had positive experiences with counseling can be a good resource.

- *Whenever possible, have a brief conversation with potential counselors before you make an appointment.* Speaking with a counselor before you make an appointment provides a good opportunity to sense whether you or your teen will be able to find a sense of rapport with them.

- *Ask the right questions in your brief phone call.* Ask about the counselor's experience with your teen's specific issue or issues. Ask about cost up front. Look at the phone call as if you are interviewing the counselor, rather than just getting help for your teen. Briefly state your teen's issue, but focus on getting to know the counselor.

- *Evaluate after the first or second session.* Make your longer-term decision after you have met with the counselor once or twice. Typically, there is a big difference between a few sessions of receiving wisdom and long-term therapy. So evaluate whether you can see yourself or your teen spending numerous sessions with this counselor.

## RESIDENTIAL FACILITIES

Excellent residential facilities are available for struggling teenagers, but they are not quick fixes. In most cases, a residential facility should be considered as a last resort after other sound options have failed.

If your teenager is totally out of control and experiencing ongoing self-destructive behavior, it is time to consider a change of environment and an extreme intervention. Most teen boarding and rehabilitation facilities are expensive, but they often do a good job. It's difficult to make good decisions in the face of a crisis, so I suggest doing your homework on residential programs early on when you see your teen starting to demonstrate some out-of-control behavior. Here are some questions to ask of potential residential facilities:

- Does the program specialize in your teen's key problem? For example, if your teen has an eating disorder, look for programs that specialize in addressing eating disorders.

- Do you want a rehabilitation center that is centered on the Christian faith?

- What educational components are a part of the residential facility program?

- Does the program offer a customized family training element and a parental support system?

- How much does it cost?

- Are any parts of treatment covered by insurance?

Make a list of facility options. Do your homework. Ask lots of questions. Speak to parents who have sent their kids to the facility you are considering, and also look at the people who endorse the program.

## "HOW ARE THE CHILDREN?"

The fearless Maasai warriors of Africa greet each other with an interesting question: "How are the children?" The traditional response carries a lot of meaning: "All the children are well." Their commitment to caring for the young members of their community is strong.

Could we say that the children are well in our society today? Frankly, until all kids are free from abuse and addiction, we must do everything in our power to come alongside them. It has never been easier for teenagers to slip through the cracks of society. With various addictions so prevalent, lots of kids are hurting and making poor choices. Parents feel the pain, guilt, and despair when their teens are suffering.

The good news is that no matter what the issue, hope and transformation can be just around the corner. Don't suffer in silence. Seek whatever help you need for this journey. And remember: *Never* give up on someone. Miracles happen every day.

 **REFLECTION QUESTIONS**

1. After reading this chapter, what concepts, ideas, or anecdotes resonated with you the most? Why?

2. If you currently have a troubled teen, to what extent are you carrying the burden alone? To what extent are you sharing your burden with others? To what extent could you be more proactive in enlisting others to help "hold your arms up" during this season of life?

3. If you do not have a troubled teen at home, what do you feel could be the issue or issues most likely to sidetrack your teen? What proactive steps can you

take now to help prevent your teen from being negatively affected by these issues?

4. Do you know parents with a troubled teen? If so,
   what are some practical steps you can take to support
   them?

5. What can you learn from others' experiences that
   might help you protect your own teen?

# PART TWO

# Common Teen Issues and What Parents Can Do

*T*HIS IS NOT MEANT TO BE AN EXHAUSTIVE list of common teen issues. If you have any concern about your teenager's behavior, there are answers for most every issue. I have found that the Internet is good place to start, but nothing beats talking about your concerns with a counselor, pastor, youth worker, medical doctor, or a mentor who has been through the stage of teenagers in which you now find yourself parenting.

# 12

# Bullying and Cyberbullying

*B*ULLYING IS PART OF THE cultural landscape for adolescents today, as it has been in previous generations. Some teenagers are still bullied in person—a 2014 study found that while in-school bullying among teens has been decreasing over time, ten percent of students have been bullied at school.[1] But methods of bullying have expanded into digital spaces as well. Through texting and social media, cyberbullying has grown and become well-publicized. Since we didn't have to contend with cyberbullying growing up, we need to guard against insensitivity to what kids today consider a major issue. It's vital that parents understand cyberbullying and find ways to protect children from it.

## WHAT IS CYBERBULLYING?

Cyberbullying takes a variety of forms, but it normally includes the use of negative, inappropriate, or threatening text messages and social media posts. Additionally, some cyberbullies impersonate someone, creating posts to cause trouble for them. Others pose as friends in order to coax personal information or images from a teen with the intent to broadcast the information in order to embarrass or cause pain. Sadly, victims of bullying often become the people who resort to cyberbullying. Why? While kids who have been physically bullied are often intimidated enough to refrain from retaliating physically, cyberbullying eliminates the intimidation factor.

Cyberbullying is extremely common. A 2014 McAfee study revealed that 87 percent of youths have witnessed cyberbullying, and 49 percent of students have regretted something they have posted online.[2] Girls more often resort to cyberbullying, while guys still rule the physical bullying world on playgrounds and in school hallways.[3] Because cyberbullying has thoroughly transformed the nature of bullying, it's important for parents to understand why it is so insidious and harmful.

- Cyberbullying can take place around the clock.

- Cyberbullying is rarely an incident between the bully and the victim only. A bully's threats, lies, and put-downs can be posted online and passed along to everyone and anyone. There is no safe haven from a bully.

- Cyberbullying is more difficult to stop. When a bully posts something threatening or demeaning, others often redistribute the post, which exponentially extends its reach. It's impossible to completely delete these posts from cyberspace. As a result, victims of bullying live in fear, not knowing when the next incident will take place or who will see the derogatory posts.

- Today, the stakes are much higher for the bullied. It's not unusual for victims to experience isolation, depression, or even to commit suicide.

- Today, the stakes are higher for bullies. Because of the widespread (and sometimes tragic) damage bullying can inflict, it is not unusual for bullies to be criminally prosecuted for their bullying behaviors.

- Today, the stakes are higher for parents. For parents of bullies, prosecutors may look for circumstances that would allow them to pin criminal responsibility for the bully's behavior on his or her parents. For families of bullying victims, the havoc wreaked can be devastating, especially for those who have lost a child to suicide.

## WHAT PARENTS CAN DO ABOUT CYBERBULLYING

- Educate yourself about devices and apps that teenagers use for communication. Take time to learn about texting, messaging apps, and social media. Learn what security measures are available for your teen's devices and apps to help block unwanted and inappropriate messages from being delivered.

- Set ground rules with your family about digital communications. Give kids clear guidelines on acceptable and unacceptable uses for communicating with devices and apps. Determine what kinds of personal information are acceptable for your kids to share. Have them agree to report to you any inappropriate communications they receive or find about themselves posted on social media sites. Setting expectations for how your kids communicate with others will help prevent your kids from becoming cyberbullies.

- If your child receives or finds a negative message about him or herself once, don't overreact. Any kid can become the object of a one-time prank. Keep your eye on the situation, but don't jump into action unless the message threatens physical harm.

## IF YOUR CHILD BECOMES THE TARGET
## OF REPEATED CYBERBULLYING

- Be sure to talk with your child. See if they know or can guess who is responsible for the cyberbullying. Check with her to see how she is emotionally handling the abuse. Give support and provide help whenever needed. Reinforce your expectation that she is not to retaliate by becoming a cyberbully.

- If you are unable to identify the cyberbully, block messages through device and app settings. If the negative messages are being virally passed online, report the abuse to the social media app's or website's management. For example, if an inappropriate image is posted on Instagram, contact Instagram directly about the image's content and what profile it appears on.

- Notify school officials. Some states and localities now allow schools to address cyberbullying even when it happens off campus. Even if your local school does not, school officials are generally familiar with dealing with cyberbullying on campus. Notification will allow them be attentive to the situation, and it's possible that they will have insights into how to help your specific situation, particularly if they are currently dealing with the cyberbully.

- If cyberbullying includes physical threats, notify local law enforcement authorities. Don't delay. Print out a copy of the threatening content, and take it with you to give to the authorities. The actual content of cyberbullying will determine where to report the crime. You can visit stopcyberbullying .gov to get the latest information.

- When in doubt, report it! If you are unsure what to do about your child being cyberbullied, report it. Whether you start with social media or other website management, school authorities, or the police, most people will help point you in the right direction if they aren't prepared or able to help you directly. But if cyberbullying is not addressed, the abuse will likely continue, and this greatly raises the risks to your child—both in their reaction to the abuse and in the potential for retaliation.

In the end, like so many other issues in parenting, you set the pace when it comes to dealing with cyberbullies. Dealing with the issue calmly, intentionally, and in a God-honoring way sets an important example for your teen.

# 13

# *Dating Violence*

*I*N RECENT YEARS, awareness of teen dating violence has increased markedly. Sadly, dating violence has become a pervasive adolescent issue. Experts define dating violence as not just physical abuse, but also emotional, sexual, or psychological abuse. Although not an exhaustive list, dating violence behaviors can include hitting, slapping, pinching, hair-pulling, non-consensual sexual activity, rape, controlling behaviors, stalking, tracking whereabouts, outbursts of rage, demonstrations of jealousy, yelling, screaming, or name calling.

In the past it was common to frame dating violence as abuse largely committed by males toward females. But recent studies indicate that this is a misunderstanding. Nearly one in five female *and* male teens say they have been victims of physical and sexual abuse in dating relationships. And when pinpointing psychological abuse, researchers have found the percentages jump remarkably to more than 60 percent of both female and male teens. Shockingly, the number of female and male teens admitting to being both perpetrators *and* victims of psychological abuse is 60 percent![1]

With dating violence occurring both in person and through digital media, it is estimated that twenty-five million teenagers in the United States are victims of abuse, and some twenty-three million teenagers are perpetrators of abuse.[2]

## WHAT PARENTS CAN DO ABOUT DATING VIOLENCE

- *Talk with your teen about healthy dating relationships.* I addressed dating in more detail in the chapter about healthy sexuality. Be sure to have a discussion with your teen on the importance of respect in a dating relationship so that she can recognize quickly if she is not being shown the respect she deserves.

- *Get to know your teen's date.* Get to know your teen's date by being friendly and asking appropriate questions. The more you know about who your teen is dating, the better you will be able to perceive what type of person he or she is. If your teen's date makes you feel uncomfortable, don't overreact, but don't ignore your gut feelings either. Share your concerns with your teen.

- *Make your teen aware of behaviors that would be considered dating violence.* Some teens may not naturally grasp the nuances of emotional and psychological abuse. Discuss these types of behaviors with your teen.

- *Help your teen understand that abuse doesn't get better over time.* If dating violence does not stop immediately, it will almost always progress to more extreme forms of abuse.

# 14

# *Depression*

**DEPRESSION IS THE MOST COMMON** mental health disorder in the United States among teens. In 2014, 2.8 million adolescents (11.4 percent of the US population between ages twelve and seventeen) experienced at least one major depressive episode,[1] with an estimated 10 to 15 percent of teenagers having some symptoms of depression at any one time. Sadly, of teens diagnosed with depression, 68 percent receive no follow-up assessment, and 36 percent receive no treatment whatsoever for their situation.[2] Unfortunately, this lack of treatment leads kids to self-medicate with drugs and is also influencing the rising adolescent suicide rate. Parents must take all teen depression seriously. If you have any questions or concerns about your child's mental and emotional health, seek the help you need to get the right advice.

Many factors contribute to teen depression. In addition to physiological factors, environmental factors also contribute. Bullying and cyberbullying, social media overuse, early puberty, stress, obesity, concussions, poor sleep habits, drug and alcohol use, and not getting enough exercise have all been linked to teen depression.

Young people experience different types of depression than adults do. Your teen may have reactive depression, a common form of mood disorder, which tends to be the least serious. Bipolar depression on the other hand, which is characterized by extreme mood swings, is more serious. Your job is not to serve as the physician or therapist but to seek the right help for your child. Getting a proper diagnosis early is always helpful. The behavior of depressed kids can be different from that of depressed adults, so I'm including a list of the signs of depression for children and teens.[3]

## SIGNS OF DEPRESSION

- Decreased interest in activities or inability to enjoy favorite activities
- Frequent absences from school or poor performance in school
- Frequent sadness, tearfulness, crying
- Persistent boredom, low energy
- Low self-esteem and guilt
- Hopelessness
- Poor concentration
- Difficulty with relationships
- Social isolation, poor communication
- Increased irritability, anger, or hostility
- Talk of or efforts to run away from home
- Extreme sensitivity to rejection or failure
- A major change in eating and/or sleeping patterns
- Thoughts of suicide or expressions of self-destructive behavior

- Frequent complaints of physical ailments, such as headaches or stomachaches

Obviously, any of these signs and symptoms could mean something other than depression, but it is better to get an assessment from a professionally trained person than to wonder.

# 15

# *Dinnertime*

$\mathcal{M}$ANY FAMILIES are now making mealtime family time. Here are eight reasons why this is a great idea:

1. Kids who eat dinner with their families regularly are less likely to be involved in at-risk behaviors. A 2009 study found that children who eat dinner with their families infrequently (less than three times a week) are twice as likely to use tobacco or marijuana and almost twice as likely to use alcohol than teens who have five to seven family dinners a week.[1]

2. Families who eat dinner together regularly are more likely to have stronger, happier family relationships. As families struggle to find quantity and quality time together, dinnertime provides the opportunity for both. Teens who frequently eat dinner with their families are likelier to say they have excellent relationships with their parents, and teens who have infrequent family dinners are likelier to say they have fair or poor relationships with their parents.[2] When families hang out together and communicate, they grow stronger and healthier.

3. Kids who eat dinner with their families regularly perform better in school. According to the latest research, compared to teens who have frequent family dinners, teens who have fewer than three family dinners per week are one-and-a-half times likelier to report getting mostly Cs or lower grades in school.[3]

4. Families who eat dinner together regularly develop a stronger family identity. Additionally, this family routine establishes a sense of stability and security that provides kids with a positive environment where they can grow into healthy adults.

5. Families who eat dinner together regularly can keep in touch with each other's lives. Everyone—kids and parents alike—can keep up to date on what is going on with school, jobs, family life, and friends.

6. A regular family dinnertime provides natural opportunities for planning and problem solving. Scheduling family meeting times to discuss these issues can be difficult. A regular family mealtime can offer a natural solution to the challenge.

7. Eating dinner together fosters learning. When families who eat dinner together engage in a variety of conversation topics, learning is encouraged. Kids who are exposed to regular family discussion times learn a broader vocabulary than those who do not.

8. Kids are more likely to receive better nutrition when eating dinner regularly with their families. Family dinnertime means kids are more likely to eat a nutritionally balanced meal that is lower in sugar and fat than if they prepare or purchase meals on their own.

Some might shy away from regular family dinners because life is busy and a family meal requires time. But the latest research shows that the average family meal lasts just thirty-five minutes. That's not a lot of time, and every minute provides great benefits for your family!

# 16

# *Driving*

*O*BTAINING A DRIVER'S LICENSE is still one of the more anticipated rites of passage for adolescents, but in recent years fewer teens have been getting their driver's licenses. A Federal Highway Administration report with data from 2014 found that there were fewer 16-year-old drivers in the United States than at any other time since the 1960s.[1] The trend though may be moving back toward a pro-driving stance—a recent study found that 92 percent of Generation Z teens plan to own a vehicle and 97 percent plan to get a driver's license.[2]

Teen driving is one of the most overlooked dangers our kids face.[3] On the one hand, a driver's license signifies an end to the endless chauffeuring that is a hallmark of kids' younger years, and this brings some welcome relief to parents. On the other hand, teen driving leads to no shortage of anxiety about the dangers than come with inexperienced drivers.

## HOW PARENTS CAN KEEP TEEN DRIVERS SAFE

While there is no guarantee your teen can avoid being involved in an accident while driving or while riding in a car being driven by another teen, you can help minimize the risks involved. Here's how:

1. *Be intentional.* Develop a plan for keeping your teen driver safe and implement it. Don't just assume that everything will work out okay without a plan in place. Don't put it off. Because the risks involved in teen driving are so daunting, being intentional about a plan is the only reasonable way to minimize the risks.

2. *Set clear expectations and consequences.* This is one area of parenting that your teen's safety, perhaps even his life and the lives of his friends, depends on. Sit down with your teen and hash out the details together. Some areas for setting limits include:

   ○ *Driving permission.* When will it be okay for your teen to drive? When will it not be okay? Some states limit teen driving during certain hours, so know what your state requires. Late afternoon, evening, and night driving carry higher risks for teen drivers. Seek to minimize driving during these times as much as possible. Set standards for your teen riding along in other teen-driven vehicles as well.

   ○ *Who can go along?* Many states use a graduated licensing system that prohibits and/or limits when teens can drive with other teenagers in the vehicle. Make sure you know and follow your state's laws. You might even choose to place your own tougher limits than your state requires because distracted driving is such a huge contributor to car crashes among all age groups. Teen drivers are six times more likely to have a serious driving incident when there are loud conversations in the vehicle, and the need to hard brake the vehicle doubles when there are rowdy passengers on board.[4]

   ○ *Notification.* Do you want your teen to notify you before she gets behind the wheel? How about when she is going to ride in a vehicle driven by another teen? Do you want to be notified when your teen arrives at the destination? All of these issues should be considered and determined ahead of time.

- *Speeding.* Obviously you don't want your teen driver to speed. That's a given. Yet, the reality is that 71 percent of teens admit to speeding.[5] So what will happen if they are caught violating the speed limit?

- *Risky driving.* This is another obvious no-no. Understand, however, that your teen's brain is wired for risk-taking, and at the urging of other teen passengers, his otherwise good judgment can go out the window.[6] Of course, you don't want him or his passengers to go out the window in a crash, so by all means, discuss your expectations for risky driving before he gets his driver's license.

- *Smartphone use.* In recent years, many states have limited or prohibited use of smartphones while driving, so be aware of what your state's laws require. I suggest a policy of not allowing teens to use smartphones while driving. Period. This means no receiving calls (even from you), no placing calls (even to you), no checking notifications and social media, and no composing, reading, or sending text messages. FOMO ("fear of missing out") is not an adequate reason for threatening one's own life and the lives of others.[7]

- *Alcohol/drug usage.* This is another obvious "not allowed." Any violation should give rise to an appropriately severe consequence.

- *Seat belt usage.* No seatbelt, no driving, no exceptions. That is the best policy and, in many states, the law.

3. *Practice, practice, practice.* Driving skills are improved through driving experience. Don't rush the process. The driver's license can wait awhile. Make sure you give your teen hours and hours (some experts suggest between fifty and a hundred hours over a six-month period) of driving practice supervised by you or another responsible adult.

## CREATE A CAR-DRIVING CONTRACT

Teens need expressed expectations, and driving is no exception. On the next page is a sample contract adapted from a "Dear Abby" column years ago.

# Driving Contract

I,_____, agree to the following "rules of the road." If at any time I violate this agreement, my driving privileges will be forfeited.

- *Traffic tickets:* I agree to pay all traffic violations on time and to pay for any increase in my insurance premiums.

- *Accidents:* If I am in an accident or damage the car, I agree to pay for all damages not covered by insurance.

- *Drinking or drug use:* At no time will I ever drink alcohol or use drugs while driving. There will be no alcohol or drugs in the car ever. I will not let anyone into my car who has been drinking unless my parents have approved it.

- *Passengers:* I will never allow more passengers in the car than there are seat belts for, and I will never allow a stranger in the car. I will not pick up hitchhikers.

- *Car cleanliness:* I will be responsible to keep the car clean and to check the gas and oil regularly.

Signed,_____

Parents_____

# Drug and Alcohol Use and Abuse

$\mathcal{M}$ANY, PERHAPS MOST, teenagers experiment with drugs and alcohol. This doesn't mean they will become addicts, but the experimental behavior that occurs at adolescence can quickly bring problems, even deadly ones, to a family. The Franklin family lost their son, the school's quarterback and a leader of their church's youth group, in a drunk driving incident the first time he tried driving after a few beers. Another set of parents is still dealing with fallout from their daughter Jasmine's drug use. Jasmine says it started because everyone else at school was trying marijuana. She smoked a joint because of peer pressure but liked it so much she couldn't stop and ended up in rehab.

No matter what your family is like, drugs and alcohol are at your teen's doorstep. In this brief section, I can't address all the issues, but I'll tackle a few. To start with, parents must be aware of what are called gateway drugs—substances that often lead to more dangerous drug use. The gateway to abuse is wide and attractive with this generation of teens.

*Beer and wine.* This is where most kids begin. Typically, they find the beer and wine in their homes or their friends' homes. The average first drink of alcohol occurs at about age twelve. Exposure to alcohol and frequency of consumption increase as teens get older. In 2015, the Monitoring the Future Survey reported that 26 percent of eighth graders had tried alcohol and 10 percent drank in the month preceding the survey.[1] If teens continue drinking alcohol, they will likely move through the gateway and experiment with the next drug.

*Nicotine.* Nicotine is one of the stronger addictive drugs known to humankind. In the United States, the prevalence of teen smoking has declined substantially over the past decade. In 2015, just 13 percent of eighth graders had smoked a cigarette, and 3.6 percent had smoked in the past month.[2] This is good news for parents. Still, the emergence of the e-cigarette gives cause for concern because it is poised to become a gateway drug in its own right. A CDC report finds that e-cigarette use among high school students in the past four years has increased tenfold, from 1.5 percent in 2011 to 16 percent in 2015.[3] Cigarette smokers are more likely to move on and try marijuana than non-smokers. If a teen doesn't try cigarettes, there is only a 20 percent chance that they will ever smoke marijuana.

*Marijuana and harder alcohol.* Due to changes in growing techniques, marijuana is more potent today than in previous generations. Research has found that the psychoactive chemical (THC) found in marijuana is at least three times stronger than in the 1980s.[4] Though infrequently reported, pot can also be laced with other drugs. Marijuana is known to produce "a-motivational" syndrome, which means the brain becomes lazy and lethargic. And similar to alcohol, marijuana affects a user's ability to make good decisions. Marijuana use can have lasting effects on the developing brain, so the consequences for teens are especially negative.

*Harder alcohol* (stronger than beer and wine) is also considered a gateway drug because alcohol is a mood- and mind-altering substance. Many people don't understand that there is a biological predisposition toward alcoholism. If alcoholism is in your family system, there is a greater chance that you (and your teens) may become alcoholics. Because alcoholism is prevalent in my family system, I choose not to drink and have made sure my children understand their increased risk of alcoholism too. Marijuana and harder alcohol use makes it easier for teens to move to the next gateway.

*Harder drugs.* Kids today are experimenting with all types of even more dangerous drugs. The following is not meant to be all-inclusive, but parents must be aware of the different drugs teens are using:

- *Club drugs* are popular at teen parties. These tend to be stimulants and even psychedelic drugs. Examples include ecstasy, Rohypnol, and ketamine.

- *Hallucinogens* distort a person's perception of reality. Examples include PCP, LSD, and mescaline. Use of synthetic cannabinoids (misleadingly called "synthetic marijuana" at times) has increased among teens in recent years. These psychoactive chemicals are made in laboratories and then sprayed on plant material so that they may be smoked. But they are not "natural." Many synthetics are extremely potent and their mind-altering affects can be highly unpredictable and even life-threatening.

- *Inhalants* are substances that people often don't consider drugs at first glance. However, they are considered addictive, and kids use them to get high. Spray paint, hair spray, and even vegetable oil sprays are some inhalants used today.

- *Prescription drugs*, of course, are found in many homes' medicine cabinets. Today, kids will try "pharming" at parties by experimenting with someone else's prescription drugs, including Ritalin, OxyContin, and Vicodin.

- *Cocaine, meth, and heroin* are three of the most popular drugs with teens when they move on to the stronger stuff. I am currently hearing about a general resurgence of heroin use, addiction, overdoses, and deaths across North America, and these reports often involve teens. If your teen is experimenting with any of these dangerous drugs, do everything in your power to get him the help he needs before it is too late.

## IDENTIFYING THE WARNING SIGNS OF DRUG ABUSE

With teenagers, it's not always easy to tell if they are in a crisis or just having a bad day. If you suspect your teenager is having trouble with drugs or alcohol, it's crucial that you take a close look to help determine the causes of your suspicions. What you find may reveal that your teenager is simply riding on the roller coaster of adolescence. On the other hand, you may find that your son or daughter needs significant help.

*Subtle symptoms of drug abuse.* The following symptoms could point to problems other than drug abuse. But together, they indicate problems needing professional treatment. If every symptom describes your teen, please take immediate action. If only a few symptoms are present, they could reflect common aspects of the teenage years. I suggest that you at least discuss your concerns with your child.

- Secrecy
- Changes in friends
- Increased isolation
- Change in interests or activities
- Drop in grades
- Getting fired from an after-school job
- Changes in behavior around the home
- Staying out all night
- Possession of a bottle of eye drops (to counter bloodshot eyes)
- Sudden change in diet that includes sweets and junk food (many drugs give users cravings or "the munchies")

*Not-so-subtle symptoms of drug abuse.* The following symptoms indicate chemical abuse. If several of these symptoms are present, you should take action immediately before the problem develops into addiction or becomes life-threatening.

- Depression
- Extreme withdrawal from the family
- Increased, unexplained absenteeism from school
- Change from active involvement to little or no involvement in church activities
- Increase in mysterious phone calls or text messages that produce a frantic reaction
- Starting smoking
- Money problems
- Extreme weight loss or gain

- Appearance of new friends who are older than your teen
- Expulsion from school
- Rebellious and argumentative behavior
- Listening to music with pro-drug lyrics
- Acting disconnected or spacey
- Attempting to change the subject or skirt the issue when asked about drug or alcohol use
- Changing the word *party* from a noun to a verb
- Discussing times in the future when she will be allowed to drink legally
- Long periods spent in the bathroom
- Burnt holes in clothes or furniture

***Surefire indicators of drug abuse.*** When the following signs are noticeable, you should have no question in your mind that your child is abusing drugs or alcohol. These are signals that the problem has not just started but has existed for some time. Intervention is necessary if the following symptoms are present.

- Drug paraphernalia found in the bedroom
- Possession of large amounts of drugs
- Possession of large amounts of money (usually indicates selling drugs in addition to using)
- Needle marks on the arms, or wearing clothing that prevents you from seeing the arms
- Valuables disappearing from the house
- Arrests due to alcohol- or drug-related incidents
- Repeatedly bloodshot eyes

- Uncontrollable bursts of laughter for no apparent reason
- A runny or itchy nose that is not attributable to allergies or a cold (a red nose would also be an indicator)
- Dilated or pinpoint pupils
- Puffy or droopy eyelids that partially hang over the iris
- Unmistakable behaviors associated with being under the influence of drugs or alcohol
- Mention of suicide or an attempt at suicide
- Disappearance or dilution of bottles in the liquor cabinet
- Time spent with people you know use drugs or alcohol
- Medicines disappearing from the medicine cabinet
- Defending peers' rights to use drugs or alcohol

## WHAT PARENTS CAN DO REGARDING DRUGS AND ALCOHOL

Much can be written that space does not allow for me to include here in this section. Many good resources for parents can be found online. One I recommend is the website for the Partnership for Drug-Free Kids (www.drugfree.org).

Here are a few general suggestions as you seek to help your kids avoid drug and alcohol use and abuse.

- *Move beyond the "not my kid" syndrome.* It's easy to convince yourself that your kids won't get involved in drug and alcohol experimentation. And you'd be wrong. *Really good kids* use drugs and alcohol for the first time every day. All kids think about trying at-risk behaviors and are susceptible to temptations and peer pressure. It *can* happen to your kids.

- *Discuss drugs and alcohol with your teens.* Talk about the dangers and potential consequences of drug and alcohol use with your kids. You may think these are not a problem for your teenager, and they may not be, but the safest course of action to protect him is to use an ounce of prevention by making drug and alcohol use a topic of discussion with him.

- *Be a good role model for drug and alcohol use.* If you are concerned about the example you are setting for your teenager regarding drugs and alcohol, it's likely that you need to make some changes in your own life. Don't forget, you set the pace for your kids.

- *Safeguard prescription drugs in your home.* If you keep your family's prescription drugs under lock and key, your teen will be safer and won't be as tempted to abuse or distribute them to others. Sure, it's more of a pain for you as a parent to play the role of family pharmacist, but get over it, for your teen's sake.

# 18

# *Eating Disorders*

*O*NE OF THE MOST COMMON PROBLEMS affecting teens, especially girls, is eating disorders. Perhaps surprisingly, anorexia, bulimia, and other eating disorders are often issues faced by good kids. These are not the teens who are using drugs, alcohol, or sex to medicate their pain. These are usually the kids who are getting excellent grades and truly want to please their parents.

So much about eating disorders is linked to self-image, and particularly a distorted body image. While I applaud organizations and companies that have mobilized to expand what is recognized by our culture as beauty, youth culture still encourages girls and guys to live up to a slim body type that most people can't attain. Our culture often talks about obesity and weight gain as a problem, yet there are over ten million women and one million men suffering from either bulimia (binging and purging) or anorexia nervosa (a deep fear of gaining weight). Both bulimia and anorexia can be life threatening, and parents must take these issues seriously.

An *eating disorder* is a term used by medical professionals to describe a person's obsession with food, weight, or inappropriate eating behavior. Anorexia is often regarded as an emotional disorder involving self-starvation that produces a very thin body and leads to heart problems, osteoporosis, changes to the brain, and other health problems. Bulimia is generally a pattern of binging and then purging food, either through self-induced vomiting or the use of laxatives and diuretics. Bulimia can be very addictive and cause many health risks as well.

Take time to become aware of the symptoms of anorexia and bulimia. The following lists are not complete, but if you notice that your teen has even a few of these symptoms, seek help immediately from a healthcare professional.

## SYMPTOMS OF ANOREXIA NERVOSA

- Dramatic weight loss with no evident physical illness
- Excessive exercise
- Preoccupation with food, calories, nutrition, or cooking
- Feeling "fat" when not obese
- Refusal to eat or eating only small amounts
- Loss of menstrual period in girls
- Thinness to the point of emaciation
- Distorted body image
- Strange obsession with food rituals
- Frequent weighing
- Perfectionism

## SYMPTOMS OF BULIMIA

- Binging and purging food
- Overeating and then spending an extreme amount of time in the bathroom

- Being secretive about food and disappearing to the bathroom after a meal
- Feeling out of control
- Emotional instability or impulsivity
- Depression and mood swings
- Dental problems
- Feeling guilty about eating, with an obsessive focus on weight and body image

Parents can't afford to live in denial when it comes to eating disorders and their teenagers. For both their physical and mental health, too much is at stake to ignore signs and patterns. Remember, you are not your teen's best friend; you are her parent. So if you sense a problem, take action. It is better to be safe than sorry.

## WHAT PARENTS CAN DO IF THEY BELIEVE THEIR TEEN HAS AN EATING DISORDER

- Discuss your concerns with your teenager. She may deny that she has a problem even if she does have one. But be willing to lovingly confront her with the evidence of any signs and patterns you have observed.
- Almost without exception, young people who have eating disorders should see a professional counselor. Eating disorders are complex and are much greater than the average parent can handle alone.
- Take action in emergency situations. If you know your son or daughter is vomiting multiple times a day, has been passing out, or has chest pain, don't use a "wait and see" strategy. Seek medical attention immediately.

# 19

# *Overweight and Obesity*

*A*CCORDING TO THE *CENTERS FOR DISEASE CONTROL,* 69 percent of adults in the United States are overweight. In this society of inactivity and processed food, it's not a surprise that people struggle with weight issues. Teens are no exception. The CDC reports that 20.5 percent of adolescents (ages 12-19) are categorized as obese. If your teen is overweight, for his health's sake, take action. I don't intend to meddle, but if you are over- weight, you may need to do something about your own habits before you ask anything from your teen.

Overweight and obesity are complicated issues. Some kids have a family predisposition to being overweight, and others use comfort foods as a way of coping with their problems. Adolescent obesity has been linked with many health and emotional problems, such as depression, early puberty, high blood pressure, stress, and anxiety. Regardless of the situation, an overweight teen is often not a healthy teen, or she may be on the road to more physical and emo- tional problems down the road in adulthood. Just like so many other aspects of raising healthy teens, you will have to set the pace.

## WHAT PARENTS CAN DO TO HELP
## AN OVERWEIGHT TEEN

Good diet and exercise are always worth the pain. It's the pain of discipline or the pain of regret. Here are some helpful tips to consider for helping an overweight teen.

- *Denial isn't a solution.* It's not unusual for parents of an overweight teen to simply deny that a problem exists. Whether it's a matter of wishful thinking, a sense of failure as a parent, or one of resignation, denial won't help your overweight teen.

- *Nagging doesn't work.* Parents who nag their overweight teen about losing weight are not effective in creating positive results. Such nagging may actually produce the opposite results. Research has found that if parents want their teen to eat healthier, rather than badgering their teen, they must adopt healthy lifestyle habits themselves.[1]

- *Exercise is the answer.* Experts recommend that kids get sixty minutes of moderate physical activity on most, if not all, days. Don't allow your teens to veg in front of a screen for hours a day if they haven't had enough exercise. Make it fun for them and, if you can, join them for some good old-fashioned family bonding. Kids watch what their parents do, and if the parents are veteran couch potatoes, they will have a harder time encouraging their kids to exercise.

- *See that your teen gets a physical on a regular basis.* Kids grow at different rates. Your teen's doctor can determine if he is overweight or just waiting for a growth spurt to correct what may seem to be a weight issue.

- *Make good nutrition an all-family strategy.* Don't just try to help your overweight child eat more nutritious meals and portions while you eat poorly yourself. Again, role modeling is important. Involve the whole family. And don't put your teen on a diet unless your teen's physician suggests it. Good eating and proper exercise will take care of most overweight issues.

● *Teach alternative coping skills.* If your teen uses eating as a coping mechanism to deal with problems, be sure that you get involved in teaching other more positive coping strategies.

● *Make sure your teen eats breakfast.* We've probably all heard the concept that breakfast is the most important meal of the day. For kids, this is especially true. Breakfast "sets the table" for your children, providing them with the energy they need to listen, learn, and be active in their school experiences.

● *Offer your teen a wide variety of healthy foods.* Make sure that your teen has well-balanced nutrition, including grains, vegetables, fruit, low-fat dairy products, and other low-fat sources of protein, such as lean meats and beans. Pay attention to fat. These days, nutritionists are concerned not only with the amount of fat but the types of fat. Smart parents are cooking with less fat.

● *Try to limit your teen's sugar intake.* Keep an eye on the amount of sugar your child is eating. Many prepared foods have too much sugar. Watch especially the amount of sugar your child is consuming through sugar-sweetened sodas and fruit drinks. One authority on teen weight issues told me, "Parents should be more concerned about their children's sugar addiction than drugs. More deaths are caused in our lifetime from poor eating habits than drug use."

# 20

# *Self-Injury*

$S$EVENTEEN-YEAR-OLD *LAUREN WAS DESPONDENT* over breaking up with her boyfriend. She had never known pain so deep and lingering. She tried to drown her sorrow in her favorite activities, but nothing seemed to work. Even a trip to the movies turned sour when she noticed her former boyfriend with his new girlfriend watching the same film. Trying to keep her composure but hurting just the same, she inadvertently yanked the tab off her soda can. Without much thought, she pressed its sharp edge deep into the flesh of her thumb. The pain and the blood that followed unleashed what had been pent up inside of her since the relationship ended. But it also gave her something she had longed for all her life: a sense of control over her pain.

Within weeks, Lauren became a full-fledged self-injurer, or "cutter." She joined several million people in the United States who regularly injure themselves as a way of dealing with the deep pain in their lives. Cutting is the most common, but other forms of self-injury include burning, bone-breaking, and hair pulling. As you might imagine, self-injurers don't always come from stable, loving homes. It's estimated that about 50 percent have a history of physical or sexual abuse. One teenager said the physical pain she inflicted on herself helped her forget the pain of a childhood marred by sexual abuse.

Exposure to the problem has increased in the past decade, but because the issue tends to be so private, it's difficult for research to pinpoint the extent of the problem for teens. It's estimated that 90 percent of self-injurers begin their behaviors as adolescents. It's also estimated that 60 to 70 percent of self-injurers are female. Analyzing emergency room data, one study found that self-harm among adolescents is growing, with ER visits for self-inflicted injuries increasing over the period examined from 1.1 percent in 2009 to 1.6 percent in 2012.[1]

The practice of self-injury and especially cutting has become part of the adolescent landscape, and some experts say it has reached "fad" status. At an overnight party, a group of middle school girls all talked about cutting themselves. They did, but the behavior didn't stop after the party. It continued and quickly became out of control for the majority of the girls involved. Like so many other destructive behaviors, cutting is present among kids who grow up in Christian homes.

What's the appeal? Cutting is, at its core, an unhealthy method of coping. Sometimes it is associated with suicidal thoughts, but not always. Rather, it's a means of actually feeling *something*. Many teens who self-injure say they feel numbness in their lives and the cutting helps them feel something. It is a physical act with an emotional release. Beyond the emotional release, the act of self-injury gives a sense of control as well as a physical satisfaction, as doctors note that cutting releases pleasurable endorphins in the brain.

## WHAT PARENTS CAN DO ABOUT SELF-INJURY

- *Know the warning signs of self-injury.* These include:
  - Unexplained and frequent scratches, burns, or cuts
  - Scarring
  - Attempts to conceal arms and legs with clothing (such as long sleeves and pants), even in hot weather
  - Possession of numerous sharp objects
  - Increased time spent alone
- *Seek help.* If you suspect or know that your teen has been self-injuring, seek help from a mental health professional with self-injury expertise.[2] Self-injury is a complicated issue, and for successful and long-term recovery, it requires a level of assistance almost no parents are equipped to provide.

# 21

# Sexual Abuse

SEXUAL ABUSE IS A SERIOUS PROBLEM, both in North America and all around the world. In the United States, one out of three young women will be sexually abused before they become an adult. Shockingly, one recent study found that one in five females are sexually assaulted in their first year of college. Most of these are date or acquaintance rapes, and nearly all involve the consumption of alcohol. One out of five to six boys are sexually abused before adulthood.[1] Every day in this country, children are being tricked, seduced, intimidated, and forced into sexual activity with another person.

## WHAT PARENTS CAN DO TO PREVENT TEEN SEXUAL ABUSE

- *Learn as much information as possible about physical and sexual abuse.* Learn who is most likely to commit crimes of abuse and why adults abuse kids. If you have any concerns, discuss them with your loved ones. There are many websites that have preventative information about sexual abuse. A simple search will turn up many of these resources.[2]

- *Listen to and talk with your teens.* Good communication is the most important principle in keeping teens safe from sexual abuse. Work to create a climate in your home in which your teen is able to share about things they may be afraid or embarrassed about. Share what you know about sexual abuse and how to prevent it. For instance, be sure your teen knows basic information like, "No one has the right to touch your body without your permission."

- *Teach your teen personal safety rules and general information on sexual abuse.* It's even better if you start when your children are younger (in an age-appropriate way) and set clear safety rules for them. Here is a list of safety rules to help you get started:

  - If you haven't done so yet, teach your kids the proper names for all their private parts; many children are not able to tell about sexual abuse because they don't know the words to use. (This discussion can be done in combination with your ongoing conversations with your kids about sexuality.)

  - Safety rules apply to all adults, not just strangers. (Eighty percent of child sexual abuse is committed by someone known and trusted.)

  - No one has the right to touch anyone's body without permission, regardless of how much the other person says they love them, how much money the person has spent on them, or any other reason.

  - Any time physical touch makes your child uncomfortable, she has the right to say no. No one ever owes another person the right to touch them. Teach your child to trust her gut feelings. Pushing, manipulating, pressuring, exploiting, or

abusing another person is never acceptable in any relationship. Your children's bodies belong to them. It is not
okay for another person to touch their private parts.

○ It's okay to say no if someone tries to touch their body or
do things that make them feel uncomfortable, no matter
who the person is. The same goes for showing (or taking)
photos or videos.

○ If an adult or teenager has abused them in the past, it is
not their fault. It is always the offender's responsibility.

○ Your child should not keep secrets about inappropriate
touching, no matter what the offender says; if someone
touches them without permission, tell and keep telling
until someone listens!

● *Know the adults in your teen's life.* Get to know your child's
teachers, coaches, youth workers, and so on. You should know
as much as you can about the adults your child spends time
with. If you have a cautionary feeling, don't let it pass. Follow
through on your gut feelings.

● *Keep tabs on your kids.* As much as possible, know where your
kids are and who they are with. Make it a family rule that if
your child's plans change, they must notify you before they
do something or go somewhere you don't know about.

## WHAT PARENTS CAN DO TO HELP A TEEN
## WHO HAS BEEN SEXUALLY ABUSED

Victims of sexual abuse live in a world clouded by the fact that
something very horrible has happened to them. They're devastated
when it happens but are often quite grateful to have someone to

talk to about it. That's why, if your son or daughter needs to talk, you can encourage them with these facts:

- *The abuse was not their fault.* It is always the fault of the abuser. Far too many young people blame themselves for their victimization. Remove all fault from your teen. Remember this is not the time to lecture her or him.

- *It is good to talk out your feelings right now.* It's not healthy to suffer in silence. The natural tendency is to not tell anyone. The shame is so strong it often keeps kids from talking. But suffering in silence will never help them heal. The pain will continue to manifest itself in multiple ways in the young person's life. It's not easy to talk about the experience, but it is the road to recovery and help.

- *There is hope and healing available.* After experiencing this kind of trauma, many young people lose hope—yet hope is what they need to move forward. I tell kids there are millions of people who have experienced what they have experienced, and those who are willing to seek help receive the healing they need. If you can find someone who has had a similar experience and found hope and healing through seeking help, this can help your teen in a big way.

- *Get counseling for sexual abuse now, in order to prevent problems as they grow older.* If they have never talked with a counselor, seek help immediately. This is not something parents can handle on their own.

- *God cares. He really does!* Sexual abuse, as much as any trauma, brings about strong feelings of anger and questioning God. Let your child know that if Jesus wept at the death of a friend, then he weeps for their pain too. He doesn't promise to take away all our sorrow, but he does promise to walk with us through our darkest moments.

Sometimes, just hearing these assurances from the person they trust most can be the starting point of recovery for a child who has been sexually abused.

# 22

# *Sleep*

*C*OULD IT BE that adequate sleep is the "magic pill" that helps teens move through adolescence successfully into adulthood? Could it *really* be that simple? Probably not—but research does demonstrate that sleep provides teens with a protective effect against some significant adolescent issues.

My review of recent sleep research involving teens shows a fascinating connection between inadequate sleep and a broad range of issues many adolescents struggle with, including depression, suicidal thoughts, drowsiness, inattention, poor school performance, increased at-risk behaviors, bullying, unhealthy diets, headaches, moodiness, high blood pressure, obesity, increased sporting injuries, an increased rate of auto accidents, and poor decision making. I know of no other area of adolescent life that is connected with this broad a spectrum of potentially negative outcomes!

Lack of sleep is a major adolescent development problem. Today, teens are getting less sleep than ever.[1] More than 90 percent of high school students are chronically sleep-deprived.[2] It's been reported that one-third of teens fall asleep in school twice a day! In 2015, the National Sleep Foundation issued new sleep duration recommendations for tweens and teens. Children up to thirteen years of age should have nine to eleven hours of sleep per night, and teens fourteen to seventeen years of age should receive eight to ten hours of sleep each night. Many experts say it is time for parents to step in and help their children get more sleep.

Earlier bedtimes may not be the solution. Researchers have found that the developing teen brain is wired so that their natural sleep cycles trend toward going to bed later at night and getting up later in the morning. In recent years, I've seen many school districts making changes toward later school start times to make more effective use of these natural teen rhythms.

The more significant issue preventing teens from getting adequate sleep is that technology and caffeine are keeping them awake. Many teens take their phones to bed with them and text, use social media, and watch videos throughout the night. Some fear missing out on texts, chats, and notifications to the extent that they drink energy drinks to help them stay awake! Just like their parents, this generation of young people multitask into the night, and this affects their sleeping habits dramatically.

More sleep will decrease at-risk behaviors, decrease depression, and increase school success. With more sleep, kids may move back to enjoying reading in bed and slowing down the pace of their lives. Unfortunately, parents are not modeling healthy sleeping habits either. Teens that don't get adequate rest will grow up into adults who live the same way.

## WHAT PARENTS CAN DO TO HELP TEENS GET ADEQUATE SLEEP

Obviously, you cannot force your teen to sleep. But parents can take the initiative to reduce behaviors known to contribute to a lack of sleep. These include:

- *Set a nightly deadline for completion of homework.* I addressed this topic in our chapter on education, but setting homework completion deadlines will help your teen become responsible for time management. Pulling all-nighters on homework or cramming for tomorrow's final exam won't help your teen get the sleep he needs, and may actually produce poorer academic performance, not better.

- *Establish an expectation of no caffeine at night.* Work with your teen to set an appropriate time after which he is not allowed to drink coffee, caffeinated sodas, or energy drinks.

- *Set a family rule for no overnight technology/media usage.* Establish a location in your home to dock/charge all smartphones, tablets, and laptops overnight. Set a time range (like 9:00 p.m. to 6:00 a.m.) during which technology is off-limits. Many teens today have televisions, computers, and gaming consoles in their bedrooms. I simply do not think this is a good idea (for reasons beyond just the sleep issue—for one thing, it feeds the temptation to view pornography). I encourage you to relocate these items from your teen's bedroom to a more public location in the home.

# 23

# Suicide

$S$UICIDE IS THE THIRD LEADING CAUSE OF DEATH among teenagers, and the percentage of teens who have seriously considered suicide or made plans for attempting suicide has increased since 2009.[1] Suicide is the second leading cause of death among young adults. Among young teen girls, the suicide rate has increased 200 percent since 1999.[2] Suicide is obviously a subject no parent wants to ever face, but with today's growing concerns, it is vital to be aware of common issues and solutions to help your teen stay safe.

There are many myths about suicide, and sometimes even people in the helping professions hold common misunderstandings.

- *Myth 1: Suicide occurs without warning.* Actually, most suicidal people give multiple warnings. Parents tend to miss the warnings or dismiss them as, "That's just our son overreacting." Take every warning or sign seriously. Warning signs of a potential suicide are available from many trustworthy websites, including suicidology.org. Unfortunately, the ultimate warning is an attempted suicide, and as parents we want to do all we can to not reach that point.

- *Myth 2: People who talk about suicide won't do it.* The truth is, most of those who die by suicide did talk about it, but the people with whom they talked probably didn't take the warning seriously. Many parents are mistakenly afraid of mentioning the word *suicide* from fear it may give their teen the idea. If you even suspect your teen is considering suicide, ask her.

- *Myth 3: Suicidal people don't seek medical help.* Research suggests that about two-thirds of people who attempt suicide visit a doctor in the month before their attempt, and almost four in ten the week before.[3]

- *Myth 4: All suicidal people are mentally ill.* Many people believe that suicide only happens to people who are mentally ill. While many people who take their own lives do have an underlying mental health issue, most who are suicidal appear normal to those around them.

- *Myth 5: Suicidal people are totally committed to dying.* One of the most common characteristics of adolescents who are contemplating suicide is ambivalence. They have a strong desire to end their lives, but they also have a strong desire to live. You can give them hope and security, and this can easily change their mind. Teens are looking for a reason to live.

- *Myth 6: When the depression lifts, the suicide crisis is over.* Often the lifting of depression by a suicidal teen means exactly the opposite: the crisis is deepening. This lifting can mean the adolescent has finally decided to take his own life. Once the decision has been made, the depression is sometimes replaced with an almost manic feeling of euphoria.

## Warning Signs of Suicide

- Abrupt changes in personality
- The giving away of a prized possession
- A previously attempted suicide
- Talk of suicide, including comments and/or notes
- Increased use of alcohol and/or drugs
- Eating disturbances and significant weight change
- Sleeping disturbances (e.g., nightmares, insomnia)
- Withdrawal and rebelliousness
- Inability or unwillingness to communicate
- Inability to tolerate or handle frustration
- Sexual promiscuity
- Neglecting personal appearance
- Theft and/or vandalism
- Adolescent depression presenting itself behaviorally
- Exaggerated and/or extended apathy and despair
- Inactivity and boredom
- Carelessness and/or accident proneness
- An unusually long grief reaction
- Sadness and discouragement
- Hostile behavior and unruliness in school
- Neglect of academic work
- Truancy and other attendance problems
- Difficulty concentrating
- Family disruption (divorce, death)
- Running away from home
- Abrupt ending of a romance[4]

My good friend Rich Van Pelt, an expert in the field, has taught for years that what a teen needs to take his or her own life is a *time*, a *place*, and a *method*. If a teen has discussed a time, a place, and a method for killing himself, he is in a lethally dangerous phase, and parents should take this extremely seriously. Seek help immediately without any delay. If there is a plan in place, the best way to stop it is to intervene, which usually means a complete evaluation at a hospital. If your teen is suicidal, seek help immediately, and if he has discussed any suicidal method, make sure the means are taken away from him.

Suicide is a permanent solution to a temporary problem. There are times when parents are simply caught off guard. But regardless of the situation, parents who are informed can be alert to problems and seek help.

# 24

# *Tragedy*

*T*ODAY'S INSTANT ACCESS TO BREAKING NEWS through TV, the Internet, and social media has exposed our kids to acts of terrorism, school shootings, natural disasters, and other tragedies. These tragedies are devastating, not only to those involved but also to people around the world who are watching live feeds and feeling the pain and loss. You and your teen may be easily overwhelmed by all of the tragedy.

## WHAT PARENTS CAN DO TO HELP TEENS DEAL WITH TRAGEDIES

Parents have a vital role to help their kids cope with tragedy.

- *Be willing to discuss tragedies with your kids.* Because of the speed at which tragic news travels today, you should assume your teenager is aware of a crisis. Be proactive bringing up the tragedy with her. Many families have children in different age groups, and if this is the case in your home, you'll need to use age-appropriate approaches regarding tragedies. Younger children can be particularly scared by tragedies and wonder if something similar could happen to them. Ask them whether they have been thinking about the crisis and whether the situation has made them afraid. Talk with them about what has happened, answer their questions, and share your concerns.

- *Tell them the truth.* Honesty is always the best policy, but this doesn't mean that you need to share every gruesome detail of a tragedy with your kids if they aren't aware. Young teens can be frightened by such cold, hard facts, so again, be age-appropriate when talking with your kids.

- *Shelter your tweens and young teens from graphic video and pictures.* Although it's likely these images will be readily available, be aware that disturbing videos and pictures don't have to be a part of conveying the "news" of what's happening. When tragedies strike—especially in the immediate aftermath—keep the TV news programs off while your younger kids are around.

- *Reassure your kids as best you can.* Since you don't have control over where or when tragedies happen, you can't promise a child that you will protect him from any that may come. But if your kid is worried about something bad occurring, tell him how unlikely it is to happen. And of course, you can tell him, "We will do everything we can to always make sure you are safe from harm."

- *Don't ignore the spiritual issues.* If you've wondered what your teen thinks about God, you'll probably find out in the wake of a tragedy. Be prepared for questions like, "Why did God let innocent people die?" Sometimes it takes a crisis to bring those kinds of questions to the forefront. And if you don't have all of the answers, that's okay. Work to help your kids search for the answers.

- *Pray for people who have been affected by the tragedy.* If your family doesn't have a regular family prayer time, I encourage you to start one. Praying as a family for people affected by tragedy also reinforces your belief in God's love and his power to care for and heal those who have been hurt.

- *Give.* As a family, find a way to give something—anything— toward relief efforts to help those affected by a tragedy. Giving to those in need is a spiritual response. The call of Christ is the call to serve. Giving helps your teen learn to cope with tragedy by serving and helping those in need. Giving provides a teen with a tangible way to respond. Your giving does not have to be limited to money. Following a natural disaster, all kinds of supplies and food are needed to help victims.

# Conclusion

Three things amaze me,
no, four things I'll never understand—
how an eagle flies so high in the sky,
how a snake glides over a rock,
how a ship navigates the ocean,
why adolescents act the way they do.

PROVERBS 30:18-19 *THE MESSAGE*

*E*VERY TIME I READ THE PROVERB ABOVE it makes me smile.
I guess we aren't the only generation trying to figure out why teens
act the way they act. I hope that this book has given you some insight
and hope. When my own kids were going through their teens, I read
everything I could possibly read and I talked to any teen specialist
who would listen. As I mentioned in the preface, I love teens and
have worked with them all my adult life. Yet for some reason I
thought it was going to be easier with my own kids. Quickly I
realized that they had to go through the same issues as everyone else.
As I look back, books and experts did help. However, one story
stands out among the rest that gave me perspective. It was a story
about cats and dogs. I have long forgotten where it came from, but
for years I have shared it with parents at "Understanding Your
Teenager" seminars. I simply call it, "Welcome to the Cat Years."

At the risk of offending cat lovers, I'll admit I like dogs better than cats. Dogs are loyal, affectionate, easy to train, and love to please. On the other hand, my experience with cats is that they can be affectionate and loving (sort of) but almost always on *their* terms. Dogs will freely give you affection at any time. A cat must be in the right mood. At times, cats seem anti-social and hardly ever want to go on family outings. Dogs, on the other hand, are the first into the car. The more you smother a cat with attention and affection, the faster it moves away from you. Just the opposite with dogs.

Do you see where I'm going here?

In the younger years, your child was probably more like a dog. Loyal. Affectionate. Teachable. Obedient (for the most part.). Then one day, you woke up and your dog was gone and you found a cat in its bed! Entitled, inattentive. Sometimes defiant. Self-consumed. Self-absorbed. Overnight your dog had morphed into a cat!

Welcome to the cat years. The best advice I ever received was from a parent of older teenagers. When he heard that my three girls were approaching adolescence, he simply said, "I know you've spent your entire adult life working with teens. I know your PhD is in adolescence. But you will still need to buckle up for the ride of your life. It will be wonderful and it will be challenging. So enjoy the ride." He was right on the mark.

# Acknowledgments

THANK YOU . . .

**Cathy Burns,** for your amazing partnership in life and ministry. Thank you for your patience with the writing of this book and for your care and love through this season of life. I am the world's most fortunate man.

**Christy, Rebecca, and Heidi,** daughters who bring me joy every day of my life, even if you thought I was a nerd when you were teens.

**Steve Ruiz and Matt Hilton,** sons-in-law extraordinaire. I'm so glad you are both in our family.

**James Stephen Ruiz,** my first grandson and one of the great joys of my life. May this book one day help your parents figure you out as a teen.

**Cindy Ward,** you are a gift from God. Thank you!

**Jim Liebelt,** you are a friend and partner in ministry. Thank you, Jim, for all your work at HomeWord and for the wonderful research you did for this project. It's a much better book because of you.

**Tom Purcell, Rod Emery and Randy Bramel,** you don't have to do so much, and yet you do. I literally thank God for you every day.

**Greg Johnson,** you rock as an agent, and you are now a friend for life. You are appreciated and valued.

# Notes

## 1 UNDERSTANDING YOUR TEENAGER

[1]Walt Mueller, *The Space Between: A Parent's Guide to Teenage Development* (Grand Rapids: Zondervan, 2009), 18.

[2]Jeffrey Jensen Arnett, *Emerging Adulthood: The Winding Road from the Late Teens Through the Twenties*, 2nd ed. (New York: Oxford University Press, 2015).

## 2 LEARNING THE DEVELOPMENTAL STAGES OF ADOLESCENCE

[1]Barna Group, "Evangelism Is Most Effective Among Kids," October 11, 2004, www.barna.org/component/content/article/5-barna-update/45 -barna-update-sp-657/196-evangelism-is-most-effective-among-kids# .VwHhNmPR2RA.

## 3 SHAPING BEHAVIOR WITHOUT CRUSHING CHARACTER

[1]If you are looking for a healthy parenting strategy, you may want to look at *Confident Parenting* by Jim Burns or some of HomeWord's other excellent resources at www.homeword.com.

[2]Jim Burns, *Confident Parenting* (Bloomington, MN: Bethany House, 2008), 134.

[3]John Rosemond, *The Well-Behaved Child: Discipline That Really Works!* (Nashville: Thomas Nelson, 2011), 41.

[4]Foster Cline, *Parenting Teens with Love and Logic* (Colorado Springs: Piñon Press, 2006), 139-40.

## 4 ENERGIZING YOUR TEEN'S SPIRITUAL LIFE

[1]Jim Burns, *Addicted to God* (Bloomington, MN: Bethany House, 2007).

[2]James W. Fowler, *Stages of Faith: The Psychology of Human Development* (New York: HarperCollins, 1981), 117-99.

[3]For a more thorough approach to spiritual influences on teenagers, see the Search Institute study in Mark Holmen, *Building Faith at Home* (Ventura, CA: Regal Books, 2007), 26.

[4]Christian Smith and Melinda Lundquist Denton, *Soul Searching: The Religious and Spiritual Lives of American Teenagers* (New York: Oxford University Press, 2005), 56.

[5]Wayne Rice, *Generation to Generation* (Cincinnati, OH: Standard Publishing, 2010), 36.

[6]"Woman Says Prayer Helped Her Win Lottery," *Headline News Discussion Starters* (Loveland, CO: Group, 1990), 31.

[7]Jim Burns and Jeremy Lee, *Pass It On: Building a Legacy of Faith for Your Children Through Practical and Memorable Experiences* (Colorado Springs: David C. Cook Publishers, 2015).

[8]Henri J. M. Nouwen, *Making All Things New* (New York: HarperCollins, 1981), 66.

## 5 CREATING A MEDIA-SAFE HOME

[1]Media is continually evolving. By the time you read this book, it's likely some of these apps will have faded from the scene and new media types and apps will have emerged. You'll need to do some homework to stay current.

[2]"Planet of the Phones," *Economist*, February 26, 2015, www.economist.com /news/leaders/21645180-smartphone-ubiquitous-addictive-and-trans formative-planet-phones.

[3]"Teens, Social Media, and Technology Overview 2015," Pew Research Center, April 9, 2015, www.pewinternet.org/2015/04/09/teens-social-media-technology-2015.

[4]A 2016 survey from digital-media firm Defy Media found that teens and young adults watch 12.1 hours of video per week on YouTube, social media and other free online sources, and 8.8 hours per week on Netflix and other subscription services. This amounts to 2.5 times the 8.2 hours per week they spend watching television.

[5]HomeWord's Weekly Culture Update always includes the section "What's Hot?," which provides current lists of YouTube videos that are popular with teenagers and the top movies now playing.

[6]Amanda Lenhart, "Teens, Social Media, and Technology Overview 2015,"

Pew Research Center, April 9, 2015, www.pewinternet.org/2015/04/09/teens-social-media-technology-2015.

[7]Ben Thomas, "Video Games May Have Negative Effects on the Brain," *Discover Magazine*, May 20, 2015, http://blogs.discovermagazine.com/d-brief/2015/05/20/video-games-brain/#.WWfvU4Tyvcs.

[8]You'll find sample agreements in the appendix that you can use as a springboard for helping you create your own agreement with your kids.

## 6 TEACHING HEALTHY SEXUALITY

[1]"U.S. Teen Pregnancy, Birth and Abortion Rates Reach the Lowest Levels in Almost Four Decades," *Health News Digest*, April 11, 2016, www.healthnewsdigest.com/news/Teen_Health_290/U-S-teen.shtml; reporting on a Guttmacher Institute study.

[2]"U.S. Teens Waiting Longer to Have Sex: CDC," HealthDay, July 22, 2015, https://consumer.healthday.com/kids-health-information-23/adolescents-and-teen-health-news-719/u-s-teens-waiting-longer-to-have-sex-cdc-701550.html; reporting on a study published in the July 2015 issue of the CDC's *NCHS Data Brief*.

[3]Ibid.

[4]US Centers for Disease Control and Prevention, "Key Statistics from the National Survey of Family Growth," August 12, 2015, www.cdc.gov/nchs/nsfg/key_statistics/s.htm#oralsexmalefemale.

[5]US Centers for Disease Control and Prevention, "CDC Fact Sheet: Reported STDs in the United States," November 2015, www.cdc.gov/std/stats14/std-trends-508.pdf.

[6]Sara E. Forhan, Sami L. Gottlieb, Maya R. Sternberg, et al., "Prevalence of Sexually Transmitted Infections Among Female Adolescents Aged 14 to 19 in the United States," *Pediatrics* 124, no. 6 (December 2009): 1505-12.

[7]Miriam Kaufman, "Sex Education for Children: Why Parents Should Talk with Their Kids About Sex," *About Kids Health*, October 13, 2011, www.aboutkidshealth.ca/En/HealthAZ/FamilyandPeerRelations/Sexuality/Pages/Sex-Education-for-Children-Why-Parents-Should-Talk-to-their-Kids-About-Sex.aspx.

[8]Ibid.

[9]Rob D. Young, "Google: Your Teen's New Sex Ed Teacher," *Search Engine Journal*, June 5, 2011, www.searchenginejournal.com/google-your-teens-new-sex-ed-teacher/30312.

[10]The Pure Foundation series includes *Teaching Your Children Healthy Sexuality*, *The Purity Code*, *God Made Your Body*, and *How God Makes Babies*, from Bethany House Publishers (*God Made Your Body* is published by HomeWord. It can be found at www.homeword.com.)

[11]Check out my books *Teaching Your Children Healthy Sexuality* (for parents) and *The Purity Code* (for teenagers). You can find them at www.homeword.com.

[12]Jane Randel and Amy Sanchez, "Parenting in the Digital Age of Pornography," *Huffington Post*, February 26, 2016, www.huffingtonpost.com/jane-randel/parenting-in-the-digital-age-of-pornography_b_9301802.html.

[13]"The Porn Phenomenon: Facts Sheets," Barna Group, 2016, http://set freesummit.org/wp-content/uploads/2016/02/Porn-Phenomenon-Fact-Sheets.pdf (accessed June 26, 2017).

[14]Belinda Luscombe, "Porn and the Threat to Virility," *Time*, March 31, 2016, http://time.com/4277510/porn-and-the-threat-to-virility/?iid=toc_033116.

[15]Morgan Bennett, "The New Narcotic," Witherspoon Institute, October 19, 2013, www.thepublicdiscourse.com/2013/10/10846.

[16]We recommend Covenant Eyes (www.covenanteyes.com), XXX Church (www.xxxchurch.com), and iParent.tv (iparent.tv).

[17]Jeff R. Temple and HyeJeong Choi, "Longitudinal Association Between Teen Sexting and Sexual Behavior," *Pediatrics*, October 2014, http://pediatrics.aappublications.org/content/early/2014/09/30/peds.2014-1974.

[18]Heidi Strohmaier, Megan Murphy, and David Drematteo, "Youth Sexting: Prevalence Rates, Driving Motivations, and the Deterrent Effect of Legal Consequences," Sexual Research and Social Policy, September 2014.

## 7 ENDING THE HOMEWORK HASSLE
## WHILE PREPARING FOR COLLEGE

[1]John Rosemond, *Ending the Homework Hassle* (Kansas City: Andrews and McMeel, 1990).

## 8 KEEPING THE COMMUNICATION LINES OPEN

[1]John Rosemond, *The Well-Behaved Child* (Nashville: Thomas Nelson, 2009), 25.

## 9 BECOMING STUDENTS OF THE CHANGING CULTURE

[1]Selected from Tom McBride, Ron Nief, and Charles Westerberg, "Beloit College Mindset List 2020," and from previous lists. See www.beloit.edu/mindset.

## 10 FINDING INTIMACY IN YOUR MARRIAGE
## AS YOU RAISE YOUR TEEN

[1]Jim Burns and Cathy Burns, *Closer: 52 Devotions to Draw Couples Together* (Bloomington, MN: Bethany House, 2009).

[2]David Stoop, "The Couple That Prays Together," *Dr. David Stoop: Marriage and Family Matters* (blog), August 6, 2012, http://drstoop.com/the-couple -that-prays-together.

## 11 DEALING WITH A TROUBLED TEEN

[1]*Collected Poems* by Ruth Bell Graham, ©1998 The Ruth Graham Literary Trust, used by permission, all rights reserved.

[2]Many couples have different parenting styles. In situations of divorce, parents will likely have even more divergent philosophies. Do the best you can to form your parenting strategy, stick to it, and bring consistency whenever possible. Seek counsel when necessary.

## 12 BULLYING AND CYBERBULLYING

[1]J. G. Perlus, A. Brooks-Russell, J. Wang, and R. J. Iannotti, "Trends in Bullying, Physical Fighting and Weapon Carrying Among 6th- Through 10th-Grade Students from 1998 to 2010: Findings from a National Study," *American Journal of Public Health* 104, vol. 6 (June 2014): 1100-6.

[2]"2014 Teens and the Screen Study: Exploring Online Privacy, Social Networking and Cyberbullying," McAfee/Intel Security, June 3, 2014, www .mcafee.com/us/about/news/2014/q2/20140603-01.aspx.

[3]Robin Kowalski, "You Wanna Take This Online?," *Time*, August 8, 2005.

## 13 DATING VIOLENCE

[1]"Preliminary Results in Landmark National Survey on Teen Dating Violence Finds Disturbingly High Rates of Victimization and Perpetration by Both Girls and Boys," NORC at the University of Chicago, October 23, 2014, www.norc.org/NewsEventsPublications/PressReleases/Pages/prelim inary-results-in-landmark-national-survey-on-teen-dating-violence-finds -disturbingly-high-rates-of-victimization.aspx.

[2]Ibid.

## 14 DEPRESSION

[1]"Major Depression Among Adolescents," National Institute of Mental Health, September 2015, www.nimh.nih.gov/health/statistics/prevalence /major-depression-among-adolescents.shtml.

[2]"Many Depressed Teens Don't Get Follow-Up Care," HealthDay, February 1, 2016, http://consumer.healthday.com/kids-health-information-23 /adolescents-and-teen-health-news-719/too-few-depressed-teens-get -follow-up-care-study-707533.html.

[3]American Academy of Child and Adolescent Psychiatry, "The Depressed Child," *Facts for Families* 4 (July 2013), www.aacap.org/App_Themes /AACAP/docs/facts_for_families/04_the_depressed_child.pdf.

## 15 DINNERTIME

[1]National Center on Addiction and Substance Abuse at Columbia University, "The Importance of Family Dinners V," September 23, 2009, www .centeronaddiction.org/newsroom/press-releases/2009-family-dinners-v.

[2]National Center on Addiction and Substance Abuse at Columbia University, "The Importance of Family Dinners VI," September 2010, www .centeronaddiction.org/addiction-research/reports/importance-of-family -dinners-2010.

[3]National Center on Addiction and Substance Abuse at Columbia University, "The Importance of Family Dinners IV," September 2007, www .centeronaddiction.org/addiction-research/reports/importance-of-family -dinners-2007.

## 16 DRIVING

[1]John Beltz Snyder, "Why Are Teens Driving Less? The Internet, Maybe," *Autoblog*, April 8, 2016, www.autoblog.com/2016/04/08/why-are-teens -driving-less-the-internet-maybe.

[2]John Beltz Snyder, "Millennials Don't Want Cars, but Generation Z Does," *Autoblog*, March 16, 2016, www.autoblog.com/2016/03/16/generation-z -wants-cars-study.

[3]A survey from the National Safety Council found that most parents (76 percent) underestimated the risk of teens being involved in car crashes. See Tanya Mohn, "What's the Biggest Threat to Teens' Safety? It's Sitting in the Driveway," *Forbes*, October 20, 2015. www.forbes.com/sites/tanyamohn /2015/10/20/whats-the-biggest-threat-to-teens-safety-its-sitting-in-the -driveway/#12fc72f04282.

[4]See Rachael Rettner, "Teen Driving: Loud Talking and Rowdiness Are Risky Distractions," *LiveScience*, April 18, 2014, www.livescience.com/44944 -teen-driving-distractions-rowdy-passengers.html.

[5]Owen Weldon, "Study Says Teens Are Still Bad Drivers," *Digital Journal*, December 3, 2015, www.digitaljournal.com/life/driving/study-says-teens -are-still-bad-drivers/article/451235.

[6]Traci Pederson, "Teen Drivers Swayed by Risk-Accepting Riders," *Psych-Central*, February 22, 2015, https://psychcentral.com/news/2015/02/22/teen -drivers-strongly-influenced-by-risk-accepting-passengers/81496.html.

[7]Katy Steinmetz, "FOMO Is Making Teens Terrible Drivers," *Time*, August 4, 2015, http://time.com/3983112/distracted-driving-teens-smartphones.

## 17 DRUG AND ALCOHOL USE AND ABUSE

[1]"2015 Overview: Key Findings on Adolescent Drug Use," Monitoring the Future Survey 2015, The University of Michigan Institute for Social Research, http://monitoringthefuture.org/pubs/monographs/mtf-overview2015.pdf.

[2]Ibid.

[3]Tushar Singh et al., "Tobacco Use Among Middle and High School Students—United States, 2011–2015," Centers for Disease Control and Prevention, April 15, 2016, www.cdc.gov/mmwr/volumes/65/wr/mm6514a1 .htm?s_cid=mm6514a1_w.

[4]Alejandro Alba, "Marijuana Tripled in Strength in the Last 30 Years: Study," *New York Daily News*, March 23, 2015, www.nydailynews.com/news /national/marijuana-tripled-strength-30-years-study-article-1.2159590.

## 19 OVERWEIGHT AND OBESITY

[1]See Rob Payne, "Parental Nagging Won't Shift Teen Weight," Medical Xpress, January 21, 2016, http://medicalxpress.com/news/2016-01-parental -nagging-wont-shift-teen.html.

## 20 SELF-INJURY

[1]Gretchen J. Cutler et al., "Emergency Department Visits for Self-Inflicted Injuries in Adolescence," *Pediatrics* 136, no. 1 (July 2015), http://pediatrics .aappublications.org/content/136/1/28.full.

[2]S.A.F.E. (Self-Abuse Finally Ends) Alternatives is an excellent resource for self-injuring teens and their parents. For more information, visit www.self injury.com.

## 21 SEXUAL ABUSE

[1]The data in this paragraph is taken from Kate B. Carey, Sarah E. Durney, Robyn L. Shepardson, and Michael P. Carey, "Incapacitated and Forcible

Rape of College Women: Prevalence Across the First Year," *Journal of Adolescent Health* 56 (June 2015): 678-80, https://lintvwish.files.wordpress.com/2015/05/carey_jah_proof.pdf.

[2]I deal with this issue in greater detail in my books *Teaching Your Children Healthy Sexuality* (for parents), *The Purity Code* (for ages ten to fourteen), and *Accept Nothing Less* (for ages fourteen and up).

## 22 SLEEP

[1]Kathleen Doheny, "U.S. Teens Getting Less Sleep Than Ever," HealthDay, February 16, 2015, http://consumer.healthday.com/kids-health-infor mation-23/adolescents-and-teen-health-news-719/u-s-teens-getting-less -sleep-than-ever-study-finds-696477.html.

[2]Alan Mozes, "Almost All U.S. Teens Are Sleep Deprived, Study Finds," HealthDay, December 11, 2014, http://consumer.healthday.com/mental -health-information-25/behavior-health-news-56/almost-all-u-s-teens -are-sleep-deprived-study-finds-694556.html.

## 23 SUICIDE

[1]Centers for Disease Control and Prevention, "Trends in the Prevalence of Suicide-Related Behavior, National YRBSS: 1991–2013," www.cdc.gov /healthyyouth/data/yrbs/pdf/trends/us_suicide_trend_yrbs.pdf (accessed April 19, 2016).

[2]"Increase in Suicide in the United States, 1999–2014," Center for Disease Control and Prevention, National Center for Health Statistics, www.cdc .gov/nchs/products/databriefs/db241.htm (accessed April 26, 2016).

[3]Brian K. Ahmedani, "Racial/Ethnic Differences in Health Care Visits Made Before Suicide Attempt Across the United States," *Medical Care* 53, no. 5 (May 2015): 430-35.

[4]Jim Burns, *Uncommon Youth Ministry* (Ventura, CA: Gospel Light, 2008), 282.

# *About the Author*

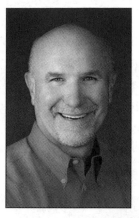

**Jim Burns** is the President of HomeWord and the Executive Director of the HomeWord Center for Youth and Family at Azusa Pacific University. Jim speaks to thousands of people around the world each year. He primarily writes and speaks on the values of HomeWord: strong marriages, confident parents, empowered kids, and healthy leaders. Some of his most popular books are *Confident Parenting*, *The Purity Code*, *Creating an Intimate Marriage*, and *Closer*. Jim and his wife, Cathy, live in Southern California and have three grown daughters, Christy, Rebecca, and Heidi.

# HOME HW WORD

## AZUSA PACIFIC UNIVERSITY

**HomeWord** seeks to advance the work of God in the world by educating, equipping, and encouraging parents and churches to build God-honoring families from generation to generation.

There is an amazing stirring amongst families and leaders today toward building strong marriages, confident parents, empowered kids and healthy leaders. It's not that family life is getting easier. Frankly, it's more complicated than ever before. However, HomeWord is uniquely positioned on the front lines and in the trenches to equip parents and restore families that are under siege.

homeword.com
facebook.com/Homeword
twitter.com/drjimburns
pinterest.com/homewordcenter
instagram.com/homewordatapu
drjimburns.com

HomeWord
PO Box 1600
San Juan Capistrano, CA 92693